PEOPLES
Anonymous

Twelve-Steps To Heal Your life

Lane W.

BALBOA.
PRESS

A DIVISION OF HAY HOUSE

All quotes from A Course in Miracles© are from the Third Edition, published in 2007, by the Foundation for Inner Peace, P.O. Box 598, Mill Valley, CA 94942--0598, www.acim.org and info@acim.org.

The excerpts from Alcoholics Anonymous are reprinted with permission of Alcoholics Anonymous World Services, Inc. ("A.A.W.S.") Permission to reprint these excerpts does not mean that A.A.W.S. has reviewed or approved the contents of this publication, or that A.A.W.S.necessarily agrees with the views expressed herein. A.A. is a program of recovery from alcoholism only–use of these excerpts in connection with programs and activities which are patterned after A.A., but which address other problems, or in any other non A.A. context, does not imply otherwise.

Balboa Press books may be ordered through booksellers or by contacting:

Balboa Press
A Division of Hay House
1663 Liberty Drive
Bloomington, IN 47403
www.balboapress.com
1 (877) 407-4847

Because of the dynamic nature of the Internet, any web addresses or links contained in this book may have changed since publication and may no longer be valid. The views expressed in this work are solely those of the author and do not necessarily reflect the views of the publisher, and the publisher hereby disclaims any responsibility for them.

The author of this book does not dispense medical advice or prescribe the use of any technique as a form of treatment for physical, emotional, or medical problems without the advice of a physician, either directly or indirectly. The intent of the author is only to offer information of a general nature to help you in your quest for emotional and spiritual well-being. In the event you use any of the information in this book for yourself, which is your constitutional right, the author and the publisher assume no responsibility for your actions.

Any people depicted in stock imagery provided by Thinkstock are models, and such images are being used for illustrative purposes only.
Certain stock imagery © Thinkstock.

Print information available on the last page.

ISBN: 978-1-5043-7049-3 (sc)
ISBN: 978-1-5043-7050-9 (hc)
ISBN: 978-1-5043-7073-8 (e)

Library of Congress Control Number: 2016919726

Balboa Press rev. date: 01/18/2017

I dedicate this book to my sweet grandmother,
Memaw, for without her unconditional love and influence,
I never would have made it. Also to my beautiful bride, Aubrey,
and my sweet little boy, Lex, who are my anchors to the Light.

Contents

Selected Awakenings and the Author's Closing Thoughts

Acknowledgments

I wish to express my sincere gratitude to Bill Wilson, the cofounder of Alcoholics Anonymous, and Helen Schucman, the instrument through which *A Course in Miracles* was received. These spiritual technologies transformed my life beyond my wildest dreams. Next, I stand in awe of my mentors, teachers, sponsors, friends and family members who spent countless frustrating hours in their attempt to help me see the light. In the many moments when I had lost all hope, they never did. I also send my heartfelt thanks to my tireless editors, Ellen, Jim and Christina. Without them, this book would never have materialized to assist in healing our world. Finally, I wish to say I love you mom and dad. Thank you for everything!

Once upon a time, there was a man walking along a beach early in the morning. The tide was out and the sun was bright with the heat bearing down, blistering the sand. The beach stretched for hundreds of miles, and it appeared that thousands of starfish had become stranded at low tide. He began throwing them back into the ocean, one at a time.

A few minutes after he began this endeavor, a stranger walked up and asked him what he was doing. He informed him that he was simply trying to save the starfish by returning them to the water.

The stranger replied, "There are hundreds of miles of beach and millions of starfish. There is no way you can make a difference."

He boldly looked the stranger in the eye, picked up a starfish, tossed it back in the water, and smiled, saying, "Well, I made a difference to that one."

There may be those who look at our world and wonder, "How can anything make a difference?"

Every starfish matters.

If Peoples Anonymous heals only one life, *we made a difference to that one.*

Preface

Welcome to Peoples Anonymous. Herein lies one of the most profound spiritual healing recipes ever entrusted to the human race. This Twelve-Step technology has the capacity to heal your life beyond anything you may have previously imagined. Millions are currently living happy, joyous, and free by simply applying this program to their daily lives.

We consider the twelve-step recipe outlined in this book to be the spiritual alchemy of the 21st Century. It transforms the lives of those who are willing to follow the directions precisely *into gold.*

If you are an alcoholic and this book has found its way into your hands, *please put it down* and go to a meeting of Alcoholics Anonymous. If you are a drug addict, put down the book and find a meeting of Narcotics Anonymous. After you have worked the Twelve Steps in one of those programs and are on a solid foundation, you may pick up this book and read it, it will enhance your recovery.

Do not attempt to use this book to get clean and sober. That is not what it's written for and there is already a *proven* program of action available for those specific conditions in AA and NA. Those programs are unparalleled in their effectiveness, and you will find the help you seek there *if* you sincerely desire recovery.

On the other hand, if you are one of the approximately 90 percent of humans who do not qualify as alcoholics or addicts and have somehow stumbled upon this book, you may be in luck. This book was written for *you*. It was designed specifically to give you access to a beautiful and powerful way of living that has become invaluable for those of us in recovery.

Peoples Anonymous proposes that anyone can significantly improve the quality of his or her life by applying the spiritual principles of the Twelve-Step Recovery Program originally given to the world by Alcoholics Anonymous in 1935.

You need not be an alcoholic or an addict to experience a powerful spiritual awakening. With this recipe for healing, radical transformation is now within your reach, *no matter your current challenges or what point you're starting from.*

By working these proven steps now available through Peoples Anonymous, you can have access to a spiritual technology that has already transformed millions of lives worldwide. You can dramatically shift your perspective and approach to life with compelling results.

Feel free to visit ***www.PeoplesAnonymous.com*** for the latest updates on the PA movement and continuing education on the application of the Twelve Steps.

Once again, welcome to Peoples Anonymous and your first step toward a significantly more amazing life.

The Human Condition

(The Problem)

The term **human condition** refers to the unique feature of simply being *human*. It can be described as an unalterable part of humanity that is inherent only to human beings and not dependent on race, gender, sexual identification, age, culture, or socioeconomic status. It includes concerns such as the meaning of life, the search for power and prestige, the sense of isolation, the pursuit of happiness, and the awareness of the inescapability of death.

Many of us in the human race suffer from some form of our own internal spiritual malady, such as always feeling *apart from, "different"* or simply never good enough. This feature of the human experience can show up as a lack of self-confidence, a sense of depression, anxiety, or merely being restless, irritable, and discontented.

At times, the human condition swings to the other extreme, creating those apparent egomaniacs that are usually covertly suffering from an extreme inferiority complex.

We often feel as though we are aimlessly moving through life devoid of a deep sense of *purpose* and *meaning*.

We of Peoples Anonymous feel that the majority of the frustration inherent in the human condition comes from (a) futilely searching for things where they are not, and (b) primarily being consumed with *self* (ego).

To medicate this internal *dis-ease*, many of us have tried some of the following: yoga, self-help books, going to counseling, seeking the "guru," retail therapy, going to ashrams, going to churches, getting sprinkled with water, taking communion, acupuncture, going to therapy, exercise, using drugs and alcohol, overeating, transcendental meditation, materialism, attention seeking, gossip, plastic surgery, neurolinguistic programming, studying theologies, taking a trip, *not* taking a trip ... ad infinitum.

We are, at times, unable to bring into our lives the *true* desires of our hearts. We have been operating out of a sense of scarcity, although we live in a universe of abundance. As Auntie Mame says, "Life's a banquet, and most poor sons-of-bitches are starving to death!"

There is a solution.

Almost none of us liked the self-searching, the leveling of our pride, the confession of shortcomings which the process requires for its successful consummation. But we saw that it really worked in others, and we had come to believe in the hopelessness and futility of life as we had been living it. When, therefore, we were approached by those in whom the problem had been solved, there was nothing left for us but to pick up the simple kit of spiritual tools laid at our feet. We have found much of heaven and we have been rocketed into a fourth dimension of existence of which we had not even dreamed. (BB p. 25)[1]

By working the Twelve Steps in our lives, we begin to seek things where they are. Coincidentally, they are much more easily found *there*. Applying this spiritual surgery to our life, we genuinely gain freedom from the bondage of the *false self* and discover our authentic Self.

We of Peoples Anonymous have found this work *heals our suffering* from the human condition at the causational level. Simply put, we now live joy-filled, abundant lives of tremendous meaning and purpose.

---

[1] BB refers to The Big Book of Alcoholics Anonymous

The Doctor's Experience

by William M. Loving, MD

Having worked with people in recovery for over thirty years, I've come to see the Twelve-Step program as a valuable tool to manage chronic dis-ease. This program makes people more humble, tolerant, content, and helpful to others. It's ironic that alcoholics and addicts, when using and out of control, are trouble for everyone including themselves, but in recovery they become better than normal.

In my psychiatric training, my analyst said, "The only thing good about being an addict or alcoholic is you *get* to go to those meetings." I would add "and use the Twelve-Step program." The program is an approach to life that follows salt-of-the-earth values and helps a person change his or her life for the better.

Step One is admitting our personal powerlessness. Steps Two and Three follow: if we are powerless, are we willing to believe in some power greater than ourselves that can help us get on track? These steps embrace humility and involve spirituality.

All of us are powerless over what life hands us. We certainly don't control fate, time, relationships, or impulses. We don't have the power to overcome certain troubles and obstacles, but we can take a spiritual approach by looking at life from a bigger perspective. Can we be humble enough to admit our powerlessness and "surrender to win," as recovery people say?

The Fourth Step reveals the resentments and conflicts in life that separate us from our Source. We all have these issues. Telling an understanding person about them (Fifth Step) helps in many ways. You don't have to go through psychoanalysis to know that getting it off your chest can help. A person gets some relief after the Fifth Step and then goes on to the action steps, Six through Nine.

When you are fully conscious and in balance, you are at Steps Ten, Eleven, and Twelve all the time. Going back through the steps on a new problem is Step Ten. The steps give you a system for dealing with everyday problems. When a recovering person encounters a new problem, you will hear him or her say, "I need to do a Fourth and Fifth Step on that." Continuing to address your spiritual life is Step Eleven, while Step Twelve is helping others or giving back. The universe works on a law that says that when you give, you get more back in return. The short version is "Give to keep."

Certainly, *everyone* can benefit from this approach to life and be a better person for it. It's a simple system based on tried and true principles for living a balanced life. It becomes its own reward. Peoples Anonymous finally opens this amazing program to everyone.

Introduction

I was relaxing in a hammock, strung between a couple of palm trees, on a small island somewhere in the Bahamas. My beautiful wife was by my side, and our precious four-year-old little boy was playing in the sand at our feet. The turquoise water, cool ocean breeze, and warm sun on my face felt like heaven.

I had decided to catch up on my writing, so out came my leather-bound journal and, as the pen hit the page, it felt like Someone gently took my hand and wrote these words: *My son, please open up this information to the rest of my kids. Thanks, Dad.*

A few moments later, a friend we'd met on the cruise sat down to join us. In the course of our conversation, my wife began to share that we were in recovery and *happened* to mention the Twelve Steps.

Our friend was a well-educated, accomplished, and fascinating woman in her sixties. She had traveled the world many times over while becoming fluent in several languages. She had great insight and wisdom from all her travels, yet she had never heard of the Twelve Steps.

With genuine curiosity, she asked, "What are these twelve steps?"

My first thought was, *Lady, they are the reason I am lying on this beautiful beach in the Bahamas instead of sitting in a cell in a maximum-security prison.*

Fortunately, I realized that would qualify as TMI, so I decided on a gentler approach.

I simply shared with her that they were the process through which my wife and I had gotten clean and sober—and as a result of applying them precisely, our lives had been transformed beyond our wildest dreams. Not only did they produce sobriety but also they had actually healed us in ways we could never have imagined.

She was eager to learn more about the program, and we talked extensively until it was time to get back on board the ship.

Back in our cabin, I couldn't get her off my mind. I remember thinking, *There might be millions of God's kids on this planet who could benefit from this way of life but have never heard of this Divine Design for Living.* Intuitively, I knew it was time to go to work, for then, I realized *exactly* what "Dad" was referring to when it felt like He took my hand and asked me to help open this program to the rest of His kids.

While still considering how enthralled this "normal" lady was with the Twelve Steps, I flashed back to an AA meeting I had once attended in Hot Springs, Arkansas.

About halfway through the hour-long meeting, an elderly woman introduced herself to the group and began sharing powerfully. I don't remember now exactly what I was struggling with that day, but her insights helped me see things differently. When you get a lot out of someone's share in AA, you usually walk up to that person after the meeting and say, "Thanks for sharing." After telling her how much she'd inspired me, I asked, "How long have you been sober?"

I have never forgotten her simple, concise answer. This sweet, kind soul shared her story with me, and that was the seed that would later germinate on such a beautiful beach in the Bahamas and eventually sprout into the idea for this book and the movement we've named Peoples Anonymous.

"Well, son," she said, "about twenty years ago, I moved here to Hot Springs and was in search of a church to join. At that time, AA just so *happened* to meet in this old, one-room steeple church that was on my list of churches to investigate.

"Instead of a late Sunday service, I had 'accidentally' stumbled into an open AA meeting—a fact that I did not immediately realize, because the speaker was using the same type of podium as normally does a preacher."

She continued, "At first, I must admit the clothes worn by the man at the podium did seem a bit odd. But it wasn't until I heard him say God and the F-word in the same sentence that I realized I *might* not be in church. Although this specific combination of words was assuredly not my personal favorite, I must admit, the depth of his sharing was astonishing. I was amazed by his breathtaking honesty and transparency about his own shortcomings and struggles in front of a crowd of apparent strangers. Behind this speaker hung two banners with the guiding principles of AA. I quickly read the Twelve Steps to his left. Immediately, I knew they could be profoundly significant for anyone willing to work with them. Next, I read the Twelve Traditions to his right and keyed in on Tradition Three: 'The only requirement for membership is a desire to stop drinking' (BB p. 562). Well, I'd had a drink before, and felt I didn't really *need* another one. Based on that, I decided I qualified for membership and have been here ever since."

While obviously not an alcoholic, she had *instantly* connected to what I call the music of Alcoholics Anonymous. Intuitively, she could hear the beautiful spiritual harmony of recovery. She must have wondered, *Could the speaker's story be true? Could this program he was referencing really have transformed a homeless, hopeless, selfish alcoholic into the man in front of me?*

He was now an eloquent, intelligent CEO of a Fortune 500 company, a man full of life, joy, and, she felt, great compassion for others.

She thought, *Well, if it worked for him, could not this recipe—these so-called Twelve Steps—help me to overcome my own struggles and heal my life?* It could, and did.

*Not only was she enjoying twenty years of being fully
conscious but also her life had changed dramatically for
the better in all areas as a result of working the program.*

If someone who by chance went to the wrong place at the right time can work these steps and radically change her life, the same can happen for you. The season has finally arrived when we can begin reaping a full harvest of transformed lives as a result of this work. This book is a seed that may take root and open the Twelve Steps to the entire human race!

A few years before that fortuitous meeting with the woman in Hot Springs, I attended an AA convention in Abilene, Texas. That's when I heard the speaker that evening make a statement that seemed extremely grandiose (and even a bit crazy). With a straight face, he stated that he believed that the *Twelve Steps of Alcoholics Anonymous might be a part of the salvation of the world.*

In retrospect, I realize he was merely suggesting that this recipe could become an integral part of the awakening of the human race. Starting with Alcoholics Anonymous, this spiritual program has been used by more than a hundred different groups all over the world, including Emotions Anonymous, Narcotics Anonymous, Co-dependents Anonymous, Sex and Love Addicts Anonymous, Overeaters Anonymous, Gamblers Anonymous, etc. If there's an addictive problem, there seems to be a Twelve-Step program to help people recover from it. Sadly, that still leaves hundreds of millions of non-addicted people without access to the Twelve Steps.

*In Peoples Anonymous, the doors are open
to anyone who wants to live a better life.*

If you are neither an alcoholic nor an addict—but are genuinely interested in finding a better way of living—this book is for you. It will introduce you to one of the most powerful spiritual technologies ever entrusted to the human race.

Working these steps has helped millions find healing, joy, peace, connectedness, and a sense of purpose that is unparalleled. If you work them precisely as they are written, they can do the same for you. There is no qualification for PA membership other than a desire to live a better life based on spiritual principles.

One of the hypotheses of this book is that in each generation, people are given a Recipe of Awakening. Throughout the centuries, it has been known by many different names: among them might be the Tao, the Way, the Good News, the Path, etc.

In the twenty-first century, it just happens to be called the Twelve Steps.

I like to call them a *spiritual technology*. I assure you it is not because I'm highly educated or a tech geek. It is because I have a cell phone, and its operating system is considered a technology. If I want to make contact with a specific person I *must* dial ten numbers precisely in a row: area code and phone number. If I dial fewer numbers or change their order, will I connect with the person I'm trying to reach?

I'm afraid not.

Coming up with my own bright ideas and dialing at will is a perfect metaphor for how I tried to work the Twelve Steps for more than twenty years. I always wanted to dial the numbers *my way*. I would not work them in order, *precisely* as they were written. I would do the ones I wanted to do, some of the time, and that's exactly why I failed over and over again to connect to the Source.

Just like dialing a phone number, the Twelve Steps—which are really twelve clear-cut Directions—must also be followed precisely if we are to get through to the only Power that has the capacity to transform our lives.

When we acquire the *Connection* by working *all* the steps in order—and continue working Steps Ten, Eleven and Twelve on a daily basis—the Power we need manifests and helps us overcome the circumstances that brought us into the program in the first place, and as we practice this spiritual technology in our own lives, we get to help heal those around us who are *willing to do the work*.

Along the way, we discover serenity as we enjoy this new powerful way of living. This is exactly what has happened for me and for millions of others who have followed this recipe precisely in gatherings all over the world!

When I began working the steps, I had an old, raggedy, torn pair of Levi's, a white Hanes T-shirt and, literally, three quarters to my name. Essentially homeless, I was staying with a friend in Galveston, Texas. Before my most recent downfall, I'd had experience in the roofing business, so I decided to call a local roofing company for employment. Somehow, I convinced the owner to hire me over the phone.

I had no car and no ladder, and yet, a few hours later, I was given a job lead to run on the south part of the island; an elderly woman apparently had a leak around her fireplace. A friend reluctantly loaned me his bicycle to use for the estimate. I rode briskly to the address and, full of shame, hid the bike in the alley behind the customer's house. When the woman answered the door, I introduced myself and was invited inside to assess the damage on the drywall around the ceiling near the fireplace.

Informing the lady that I would be right back, I shut the front door behind me quickly. Then, I climbed a side fence to reach a tree branch that just *happened* to reach over her roof. From there, I scrambled onto the roof to discover the problem and climbed back down, somehow without breaking my neck. After I told the woman what was wrong and the cost to fix it, she graciously accepted. Immediately, I called my new boss to let him know I had sold my first appointment. The rest, as they say, is history.

Today, as the direct result of working the Twelve Steps in my life and practicing these spiritual principles in all my affairs, I live a life beyond my wildest dreams. I am married to the most beautiful woman on the planet, and a few years ago, we were entrusted with the coolest little boy, our first and only child. We own a beautiful home by the lake in Austin, Texas, and a place near the ocean in Miami Beach, Florida. The joy and beauty of my life nearly bring me to tears every time I remember that when I began this journey, I was homeless.

Starting from this humble beginning, after having also spent years in jails and institutions, made that day in the hammock extra special as I talked to my new friend from the cruise ship about the Twelve Steps and what they had done in my life.

Why PA?

Peoples Anonymous has come to the world to help remove all degrees of separation in the twelve-step movement of transformation. Prior to PA, one *could* gain access to the twelve steps through a variety of different *special interest* groups. As beautiful and powerful as these individual gatherings are, they were born in an atmosphere of separation, believing they needed to identify with a specific form of dis-ease for healing.

PA proposes we all struggle with some form of the human condition and we are all in this together. Our interests do not lie separate nor does our Healing.

It's intriguing that this recipe of awakening was initially entrusted to a group of alcoholics for its trial period. I believe this might have happened for two reasons.

First, alcoholics' lives literally depend on practicing and applying the program. Consider a quarterback handing off a football to his running back. What if, during that transfer, he warns his teammate that if he drops it or fails to make the touchdown, he will surely die, or spend the rest of his life in prison? It would completely change the game—and there might even be more touchdowns and fewer fumbles.

Before 1939, when the Twelve Steps came through Bill W., who felt inspired by God, alcoholics were dying by the thousands. *If* they survived until the latter stages of their alcoholism, they would have to be locked up in an asylum or a prison to stay sober. Before AA, there was little hope for recovery. Maybe the Universe knew that we would take good care of the program, since we would be nothing without it.

The second reason may have been to *demonstrate the power* these steps have for healing the un-healable with some of the most difficult and hopeless cases imaginable.

Nothing, absolutely nothing throughout the centuries, since man first crushed grapes, could seem to fix the alcoholic. It was, and still is, one of the most insidious, cunning, and baffling diseases ever encountered by the human race. There still seems to be no *viable* solution other than the daily reprieve offered by this recipe for transformation.

To compound the problem, one of the seeming perplexities of alcoholism is that it appears to be self-inflicted. Even now, there is still a prevailing erroneous belief that alcoholics are weak-willed and are deliberately destroying their lives. That is simply not the case. Alcoholism has always been an illness. Today, it is finally classified officially as a disease by the American Medical Association.

I like to imagine the Great Healer thinking, "If the world can see the Twelve Steps transform the lives of the vast number of hopeless, incurable alcoholics on the planet, they might easily believe it could work for them."

Well, the fact is that for eighty years, it has worked miraculously, enabling millions worldwide to live happy, clean, and sober lives. Fortuitously, it has also produced healing, joy, abundance and radical transformation beyond anything imaginable!

In the twenty-first century, the need for PA may be three-fold:

1. To open this spiritual technology and provide real-time access to the Twelve Steps to anyone sincerely interested in radically transforming his or her life (no distinguishing feature or special interest required).

2. To reintroduce the small yet vital word *precisely*. This seems be one of those lost essential ingredients that has become watered down over the years. It was originally emphasized by Bill as *part of the successful application of the Twelve Steps*—or any recipe, for that matter. If you research the effectiveness of AA, for instance, you may find some negative feedback. There is even some rhetoric actually blaming AA and/or the Twelve Steps for people's failure in the program. This is kind of like blaming a cake recipe that calls for three eggs, two cups of flour, a cup of milk, half of a tablespoon of butter, etc., for not working after *you decided to put in only half or three quarters of the ingredients*. Please forgive us, but we cannot overemphasize this truth enough.

3. There are those who advocate the "take what you want and leave the rest" approach to healing and recovery. We have not seen this yield amazing results in such things as: *not taking your medicine* as prescribed by the doctor or in failing to follow the recipe precisely in this *Program of transformation*.

We of Peoples Anonymous have never seen anyone's life fail to improve dramatically as a result of working the Twelve Steps in the exact fashion they are prescribed.

Simply put, how could trusting God *as you understand him*, cleaning house (getting your affairs in order, cleaning up the wreckage of your past) and helping others *really* fail to improve your life?

It may be impossible to scientifically ascertain the success or failure rate of any Twelve-Step program. In order to intelligently speak to this *honestly*, one would have to personally observe each person working the program and ensure that it was being worked accurately, thoroughly, and sincerely. Who is in a position to do that?

The process of working the Twelve Steps, as stated, is identical to baking a cake. If you follow the recipe exactly, you'll get a delicious cake. If you improvise, you may get a cake your dog wouldn't eat. Working the steps, likewise, requires following the recipe specifically. Some people mistakenly believe they can use part of the recipe and leave out the rest. We have seen this to be disastrous and even fatal in the case of alcoholics and addicts.

On the other hand, those of us who have applied the Twelve Steps precisely have experienced a profound spiritual awakening and a revolutionary renewal of our lives. In the beginning, all *we* wanted was release from addiction—but we stumbled into a whole new way of living. We discovered the capacity to completely heal our lives beyond anything we had previously known.

We have seen it work in the most difficult situations imaginable. It has transformed hookers into loyal wives and loving mothers, junkies into amazing fathers, crack-head criminals into practicing attorneys at law, homeless people into high-finance executives, and ex-cons into honest, valuable and productive members of society.

We have seen children who were removed from their homes by Child Protective Services due to a parent's addiction and abuse returned to healthy and humbled mothers and fathers who now understand the great gift of parenthood.

> There seems to be no amount of devastation that we have not seen entirely transformed by the miracle-working power of the Twelve-Steps.

Bill W. wrote: "Our public relations policy is based on attraction rather than promotion" (BB p. 562). The primary appeal of this program is visible in our actions, and the resulting fruit of the work is visible in our lives. Others see that we have profoundly changed and ask what has happened; this is when we get the opportunity to share our experience with the program. We of Peoples Anonymous wholeheartedly believe this program can also help *you* find your bliss and real purpose in life.

If you will summon all of your courage, humility, and willingness—while going after this work with the *desperation of a drowning man*—we assure you that the best years of your life lie ahead, no matter your present circumstances.

Fortunately, we need remove only two words from the Twelve-Step program of Alcoholics Anonymous for them to apply to anyone: *alcohol* and *alcoholics*.

If you can find your personal powerlessness—and/or the resulting unmanageability that spawns from attempting to control that which you are ultimately powerless over in any area of your life— you're ready to begin.

Welcome to Peoples Anonymous, one of the most bittersweet and profound experiences on earth. Fasten your seatbelts. You are in for one of the most exciting journeys of your life.

For the record, we absolutely *insist on enjoying the ride!*

The Twelve Steps of Peoples Anonymous

1. We admitted we were powerless—that our lives had become unmanageable.
2. We came to believe that a Power greater than ourselves could restore us to sanity.
3. We made a decision to turn our will and our lives over to the care of God *as we understood Him.*
4. We made a searching and fearless moral inventory of ourselves.
5. We admitted to God, to ourselves, and to another human being the exact nature of our wrongs.
6. We were entirely ready to have God remove all these defects of character.
7. We humbly asked Him to remove our shortcomings.
8. We made a list of all persons we had harmed and became willing to make amends to them all.
9. We made direct amends to such people wherever possible, except when to do so would injure them or others.
10. We continued to take personal inventory, and when we were wrong we promptly admitted it.
11. We sought through prayer and meditation to improve our conscious contact with God, *as we understood Him,* praying only for knowledge of His will for us and the power to carry that out.
12. Having had a spiritual awakening as the result of these steps, we tried to carry this message to others and to practice these principles in all our affairs.

CHAPTER 1

Step One

*We admitted we were powerless—that our
lives had become unmanageable.*

In its purest form, Step One is simply asking for Help.

*I*n *my weakness lies His strength.* I believe this idea may have been the genesis of the inherent truth found in the First Step. No one likes the idea of powerlessness; nor do they usually *initially* desire to ask for help. Even more appalling is the idea that our lives have become unmanageable. But the First Step is not actually implying that we have *no* power—for assuredly, we humans have some power.

On one side of the spectrum might be the example of nuclear bombs. This destructive power could end the world. On the other hand is the power of love, a source of great strength, as demonstrated by the many influential souls who have come before us. The effect of this *power* in our world is significant. From Jesus to Buddha, Gandhi to Mohammed, Martin Luther King to Mother Teresa, and through countless other great masters, we have been shown the radical, transformative power of Love.

A year ago, my sister suddenly discovered that she had cancer. In the very instant the doctor looked her in the eyes and told her the diagnosis, she fully came to terms with her personal powerlessness. She didn't have to study the First Step to learn its meaning; she learned it the hard way. We may encounter external circumstances or crises that cause us to embrace our personal powerlessness; these could be—but are not limited to—divorce, financial difficulties, illness, death of a loved one, or some other type of loss.

We then begin to awaken to the truth that there are many things in our human experience over which we are utterly powerless. We also learn, usually by trial and error, that the more we try to force our will onto that over which we actually have no power, the more powerless we become. This futile exercise appears to be one of the main ingredients in the fundamental misconception causing most of the pain in the human experience: We are "victim[s] of the delusion that we can wrest satisfaction and happiness out of this world if we only manage well" (BB, p. 61).

These *moments of truth*, disguised as difficulties, can bring us closer to recognizing that lack of power is ultimately our dilemma (BB. p. 45). We eventually come to realize that a power greater than ourselves is needed to bring about the desired result in this experience called life.

Radical Recovery begins as we practice the Shakespearean ideal, "To thine own self be true." Some of us have seized this summons like a life-preserver.

The first half of the First Step—"We admitted we were powerless"— is simply stating a fact, although it may be one of the least popular truths that underlie the human condition. Our ego rebels against this reality and will go to great extremes to deny it.

As we spin on a rock through space at approximately 67,000 miles per hour with a death sentence awaiting us, our ego tells us seductive lies. Especially when we are young, ten feet tall and bulletproof, it constantly whispers in our ear of its never-ending power and dominance over all things.

To the ego, the idea of *powerlessness* is blasphemy. This is in strict accord with the ego's basic doctrine, "Seek and do not find" (T-26. IV.1:4)[2]. The ego has us constantly looking for the power to overcome a given situation *everywhere*, except where the power actually lies. This

---

[2] Referencing A Course In Miracles

useless search—looking for things where they're not—helps maintain the life of the ego, for connecting with real Power would mean we no longer need our old "friend." This discovery would ultimately ensure its demise. No one wants to die, especially our egos.

Let us take a moment to define our use of the word *ego*.

It is simply a *false idea about who we are*, born shortly after we take our first breath. We come into this world exactly as we were Created: eternal spiritual beings, pure reflections of our Source. Way too soon, our egos spring forth, informing us that we are temporal beings—that we are guilty, that we are vulnerable, and even that we can die. As the ego grows stronger, one of its greatest fallacies is to convince us to spend our lives chasing paper with green ink on it (money), persuading us that it *actually* has value and is worthy of *spending a life* in its pursuit. The ego is constantly misleading us by causing us to value the valueless. Its mission is to have us look for things where they are not, thereby ensuring its survival.

The first half of the First Step is a shot across the bow, giving the ego notice that the gig is up. It is the beginning of the end of the fallacy of our personal omnipotence.

> **The ego would have us believe that admitting personal powerlessness is a sign of weakness or cowardice, whereas in truth, it is a formal invitation to the Great Power.**

When we humbly and honestly acknowledge our powerlessness, we gain access to His Strength. Call it the price of admission to stop living a self-propelled life and begin a deeper journey that is divinely guided.

For instance, as we become more honest with ourselves, we may uncover the fact that we do not even have the *power* to move our little fingers. If you think, *move, little finger*, and you are fortunate, it may move. However, most of us cannot explain how this happens. Somehow, the food you consumed earlier is converted into the energy you now use to move your finger. But you do not control your access to that power.

Simple lessons like these in self-honesty are very helpful in the beginning. As we realize how little we know about things, like the working of our own *hands*, we become less interested in running the world or micromanaging the lives of others. Even scientists who have studied physiology and biology for decades cannot explain the miracle of the human body. Some of us still wonder Who or what connected these thousands of miles of nerves and veins so perfectly.

Honesty is the spiritual principle of the First Step.

When we get rigorously honest with ourselves, we realize that *we do not have the power* necessary to attain the true desires of our hearts. Astonishingly though, the instant that admission is made, the Power begins to flow freely into our lives. We begin to overcome difficulties large and small that we were unable to surmount before. It is true that once we connect to the Power, this is only the beginning. There is work and still more work. We must learn to maintain, utilize, and *allow* the Power to transform our lives.

Admitting my personal powerlessness is one of the hardest things I have ever done. The idea of surrender contradicted everything I had been taught and was in direct opposition to all the ideas I had accepted on my way to becoming an adult. After all, my dear father had always said: "If there's a will, there's a way." The Sicilians and Vietnam veterans who deeply influenced my younger years made it clear: "Surrender is *not* part of the curriculum!" So, I refused, or was unable to admit, glass in hand, that I could not beat this thing!

Why humans have such a strong urge to fight their way through problems is likely tied to the survival instinct. If I were fighting a bear, that instinct would be extremely helpful, but using the fight-or-flight response to run my life and manage my affairs turned out to be catastrophic. The Power to heal my life had to come through me rather than from me. The key to my new life was unconditional surrender to a Power greater than myself.

Once, I was in a sweat lodge. This is a Native American spiritual practice during which you get on your hands and knees and crawl into an *Inipi*, an enclosed, low-ceilinged, canvas-covered teepee. Then, hot rocks are brought in and doused with water to create steam and more heat while you sing and pray.

This was one of my first lodges. As the heat increased, I became fearful and didn't know what to do. This lodge was filled mostly with full-blooded Lakota men; to tap out would have felt shameful, weak, and even dishonorable. The harder I fought internally, the hotter it became. In those final moments, as I was about to bow out and give up, *I gave up!* I surrendered unconditionally. I had my first physical experience of coming to the *end of myself*.

In the instant, I finally accepted my personal powerlessness and said, "I can't stand this one second longer." I had exhausted all of my own personal resources; in that moment of complete surrender, I suddenly felt connected to the Resource of all things.

I will never forget that life-changing experience. Indisputably, I felt a Power flow *through* me, and the heat suddenly *seemed* to diminish and become bearable. It felt as if a cool breeze began to blow on the inside, and a peace that surpassed my understanding overcame me. All was well. Not only was I able to finish the remaining time in the lodge but also I finally *understood* the surrender principle inherent in the First Step. The statement, "In my weakness lies His Strength" became *real* for me at approximately 160 degrees Fahrenheit.

Although surrender is extremely hard for most of us, there comes a time when the only thing harder than letting go is to keep holding on.

The Twelve-Step technology instructs us, right off the bat, that we *must* let go of old ideas. In his book *Power vs. Force,* David Hawkins suggests that power genuinely works better than force. While reading his exceptional work, I realized that for decades I had been using force to try to manage my life and the lives of those around me. I had been wrestling life to the ground in my attempt to produce the desired result in my affairs.

The first half of the First Step caused me to embrace a *radical* new idea: by admitting my powerlessness, I could actually plug into a Power greater than myself. It is the same Power that lights the sun, moves the planets, grows the trees, and guides the butterflies on their journey. By no longer trying to force what I *thought* I wanted in a given situation, I realized I could surrender the outcome to this process. Understanding that I usually do not want what I *think* I want, I began allowing the Higher Power to produce the results. They were often different from what I thought I wanted, but they were *always* the actual desires of my heart, not the cravings of my ego.

What occurs when we sincerely work these steps in any situation is usually far greater than anything we could have imagined. But what exactly does *working the steps* mean? And how do we apply the principle of being powerless in our lives?

We begin by getting more honest. First, we get authentic with ourselves and eventually to others. Strange as it may seem, being honest with ourselves is often the hardest part. For some strange reason, we are usually the last ones to know the most difficult truths of our lives. There is a funny saying in Alcoholics Anonymous: "There is no such thing as an *anonymous* alcoholic, except unto himself." Everyone in his or her life knows there's a problem—even the neighbor's dog. Everyone but the person with the problem.

In a way, recovered alcoholics are especially blessed, for we had a malady so painfully obvious to the world it ensured that we would be brought to our knees and ultimately to this radical spiritual way of life. (When we use the word *radical,* we are emphasizing a spiritual upheaval: the vast difference between the way we lived our lives *before* working the steps and how we live today.) Once we incorporated the spiritual principles of the steps into our lives, the difference was night and day. Our new way of life felt like we were moving from darkness into the Light.

Obviously, we can testify that the steps work for alcoholics. But what about the so-called "normal people" of the world, the *non-alcoholics* for whom this book is written? How do you get to the place where you're willing to let go of your old ideas and make drastic, radical changes?

How do you become open to a new spiritual way of life that may conflict with many deeply held beliefs and former ideas?

> There may come a time when the last thing you lost, or the next thing you are about to lose, is more important than your cherished beliefs and old ideas.

That's when we become as open-minded as only the dying can. The great writer Henry David Thoreau wrote, "The mass of men lead lives of quiet desperation." They go to the grave, as Oliver Wendell Holmes observed, "with all their music still in them."

Until we awaken, we cannot live our lives fully. Many of us experience a profound lack of joy. At the same time, we have a deep desire to live fuller, richer lives. We know that there must be a better way. This inner ache may surface when we meet someone who has found real joy by applying these spiritual principles, and we see their lives bearing fruit with our own eyes.

Dying to your old self to allow your *authentic self* to emerge can be painful. However, it is worth the struggle, just as the caterpillar labors to escape the cocoon and eventually spread its wings to fly. This dying of self usually entails realizing that we can no longer do the same thing over and over and expect different results. This is our program's definition of insanity.

Ultimately, the motivation to undergo this profound change and do this work will come from life itself. Life has a beautiful way of getting us to the place where we have had all of ourselves we can stand. This moment of clarity, the *coming to the end of self*, either in a sweat lodge or in the middle of a ferocious divorce, is one of the most powerful moments of life.

When we finally run out of "bright ideas" and become willing to *precisely follow the directions* of this proven program of action, a new life will be given to us. We can close the gap between who we are and who we were created to be—in all areas of life.

In conclusion to the first half of Step One:

We can be just as joy-drawn to the work as we can be pain-driven into it.

Many may come into the spiritual life due to suffering. It matters not why we come to Peoples Anonymous: only why we stay. Most of us remain in the interest of pure joy. The *first* half of the First Step is the simple admission that:

No problem can be solved by the same consciousness that created it. We need to see the world anew.

—Albert Einstein

The second half of the First Step introduces us to the idea that our lives have become unmanageable. Here, you might be wondering: What exactly does "my life's unmanageable" mean, and how exactly does that apply to *my* life?

First, this is not about the external struggles of your life. It is not suggesting that you can't hold down a job, pay your bills or get the things you *think* you want. It does not mean you can't finish school, get married, raise children, or perform the many tasks of daily living. However, some of us have seen the symptoms of our internal spiritual malady bleeding out into the *circumstances* of our lives/the unmanageability of our outer world. This may have included divorce, financial struggles, job loss, family turmoil, conflict with others and disharmony with friends.

These difficulties, great or small, are not the problem, but actually *symptoms* of the problem. For years, I thought the unmanageability of the second half of the First Step referred to my inability to successfully manage the people, places, and things in my life. Ironically, I felt very proficient in controlling the lives of others, while still suffering from the delusion that my happiness would be complete if they would simply do as I wished. I am ashamed to admit, I really believed I knew what was best for everyone. It was a rude awakening when I realized, *I do not perceive my own best interests* (W-pI.24.7:1).

From that moment of truth, I asked myself the next logical question: *If I cannot honestly perceive my own best interests, how can I perceive the best interests of others?*

In my frantic attempt to get all the actors on the stage I called *my life* to do as I demanded, I noticed my own perspective on life becoming more and more distorted. I began to have a hard time differentiating the true from the false. I continued to suffer from the delusion that I actually wanted what I wanted, whereas every time I spent vast amounts of energy acquiring the thing I so desperately sought after, within seconds or days at best, I was over it! How do you produce an outcome that is in the best interest of all when you don't have a clue what that is, *and* you are in the process of uncovering the conveniently hidden truth, "I don't even want what I want"? Although we may eventually see the evidence of unmanageability in our *external* lives, the second half of the First Step is largely referring to our *inner lives*.

We call this internal spiritual malady the "ism," as in alcohol-ism. It is the ego's attempt to force **I**, **S**elf, and **M**e onto the lives of others. This spiritual malady—the *ism*—is a direct result of the selfishness of the human condition and is not an exclusive feature of the alcoholic.

Peoples Anonymous helps heal *human condition–ism* through a daily program of action called the Twelve Steps.

This is the true dis-ease to which all human beings may relate. When we are brutally honest with ourselves, often we may discover that we spend way too many of our precious moments "restless, irritable, and discontented" with just about everyone and everything in our lives (BB, p. xxviii). At some point, we had lost the sense of ease and comfort in life. There was no longer peace inside of our own skin. Instead, many of us lived with a profound sadness. The more we tried to manage these feelings with such things as alcohol, drugs, shopping, religion, sex, food, or exercise, the worse things became.

In the final analysis, we realized that we could never produce the desired result, internally or externally, by attempting to force our will in our own lives or in those of others. It was especially painful to become aware of the harm we'd been causing all along.

We began to realize that we had been victims of the delusion that we could wrest satisfaction and happiness out of this world, if we could only manage well (BB, p. 61). It may not be that we worked the First Step as much as it *worked us*. We have finally awakened to the inherent truth of this powerful statement: we are powerless over our human condition, and when we attempt to manage everyone and everything, *our lives* become even more unmanageable.

"Remarkably, admitting our personal powerlessness is actually one of the most Powerful statements we can ever make" (Jack Boland).

Coming to the program, many of us suffered tremendously from the illusion of separation. We felt disconnected from those closest to us and even our Higher Power. We did not seek guidance from that Power, because we were too busy trying to *be* the power. But once the *real problem* and all of its consequences were fully accepted, we became willing to go to any lengths to find a solution. Fortuitously, we were more open to a Power greater than ourselves that could restore our lives to sanity, balance, joy, and possibly even bliss. This was the natural movement that led us into the Second Step.

Step One Exercises

1. Make a list of the people, places, and things you can identify that you are ultimately powerless over.

2. List ways in which you have noticed unmanageability in your internal and external life.

3. Write a short description of the problems in your life. This will be a road map to look back at to see how far you've come.

4. Describe in a page or less what it feels like to be you *internally*. What is it like to live inside your skin today?

5. *Pay attention* to the world around you, and notice if life brings you physical experiences to help internalize the powerlessness and unmanageability of the First Step projected on the screen you call *your life*.

How successful have you been in attempting to exert power over the many things in life in which you are powerless?

CHAPTER 2

Step Two

We came to believe that a Power greater than ourselves could restore us to sanity.

O ne useful definition of insanity in relation to the Second Step is: "Doing the same thing over and over again while expecting different results."

Am I insane?

Do I *really* need a Power greater than myself to simply live my life?

Must I reexamine this vast concept of "God"?

Where shall I start?

Here, like the proverbial elephant in the living room that no one wants to *really* talk about, or incessantly talk *only* about, this notion of God must be briefly addressed to begin Step Two. In truth, this is not the place in the process where lengthy conversations about God best fit. (Fortunately, there is a proper time and place for such discussion in Step Eleven, if you are so inclined). By then, hopefully, we will have begun to have a spiritual awakening. Then, we can draw on our *actual* experience and debate others' experiences if needed.

But for now, let's talk about the words *Power greater than ourselves.*

I do believe that when the originators of the steps penned these words, they were *hinting* at the idea of God. Yet, some of us whose lives have been transformed by this technology have observed that even though we initially had deep theological convictions—while others had agnostic or atheistic leanings—radical healing was not only about *believing in something*: the Power needed to actually co-create fundamental change in the conditions of our lives and the lives of others had to come by *doing* something rather than just *believing* something.

Here, we of Peoples Anonymous want to emphatically assure *everyone*—whether believer, agnostic, or atheist—if you have a sincere desire to heal your life, and you are willing to hold all of your fundamental ideas up to the light of doubt, you will find the truth you seek.

In our beautiful recovery movement, even the staunch atheist is afforded a front-row seat to a Power greater than himself as he *undoubtedly* witnesses the transformation of the lives around him. Even the simplest thought "Is that odd, or is that God?" will slide him through the door.

There are many *powers* much greater than ourselves that can be extremely helpful in the healing of our lives—PA or AA, for example. As a group, they have been able to accomplish what we might not have been able to bring into our lives of our *own* volition. In addition, at first, some of us considered a sponsor to be a *power greater* than ourselves (this person had begun where we were, yet he or she was now where we wanted to be). In reality, our sponsors had accessed a Power that produced a real-time demonstration of joy, recovery, and purpose in their lives.

Any authentically positive, helpful influence can be considered a power greater than ourselves if it will help us fulfill the initial requirement of the Second Step. Even the steps themselves qualify, for they have already done for millions what we are trying to accomplish for ourselves.

There is action and more action needed.

The initial shift of the Second Step is to help us begin to use our mind as a *receiver* rather than a *guidance* system.

The spiritual exercise of receiving direction *temporarily* from those who have transformed their lives helps us stop operating our own lives based on old, familiar ways of attempting to run the show. Ultimately, in the Second Step, we hope to plug into our *Source* for guidance. At the same time, during this incubation period, while we are completing the Twelve Steps, human aid and guidance are vital, though only from those who have experience with this process of transformation and *have had a profound demonstration in their lives.*

As I struggled with the idea of allowing someone to give me guidance, I remember my mentor reassuring me with these words:

"If I do my job well, you will not need me very long."

I replied, "You don't like me?"

He answered, "Actually, I do like you, but that's not the point! My job is to help lead you to your Source, and then get the hell out of your way. I am not here to allow you to become dependent on me or play middleman between you and the God of your understanding. For a very short time, I am willing to guide you through this process and help you make the important *executive decisions* that may arise while you are getting connected."

I must admit, this was radically different from the impression I had received growing up in church from my minister. Allowing another human being to give me directions, especially those that made no *sense* to me, was crazy enough, but actually following those directions was the first evidence of real change in my life.

The sponsor who helped me get sober—and hopefully stay sober this time—was twenty-four years old when we met. I had been in and out of AA almost as long as he had been alive. I was desperate and miserable while he was glowing in the dark with pure bliss. Simply put, *I wanted what he had* and eventually became willing to go to *any lengths* to get it! So, for the very first time in my life, I did as I was told.

When the words "Faith without works is dead" were originally penned, they may have reflected a forethought for this specific process of recovery; for the alcoholic, these words are appallingly true. Many great people of enormous faith have died of alcoholism. Either they didn't know of the work that had to be done for genuine recovery, or they were simply not willing or able to do what was required.

We cannot stress enough that this is a program of *action*. It is not a program of thinking, believing, talking, knowing, or wanting. The only thing that really matters and produces results with this spiritual technology is *doing*.

With this work, we move our feet, not our lips!

In the Big Book of AA, the authors wrote a chapter called "How it Works." It opens with this:

> *Rarely* have we seen a person fail who has thoroughly followed our path. Those who do not recover are people who cannot or will not completely give themselves to this simple program, usually men and women who are constitutionally incapable of being honest with themselves. There are such unfortunates. They are not at fault; they seem to have been born that way. They are naturally incapable of grasping and developing a manner of living which demands rigorous honesty. Their chances are less than average. There are those, too, who suffer from grave emotional and mental disorders, but many of them do recover if they have the capacity to be honest (BB, p. 58).

Rumor has it that Bill W. was once asked, "If you could, would you change anything about the program?" He was noted as saying, "I would change the word rarely in the chapter 'How it Works' to never."

It is also important to note, at this stage of the game, that the word *directions* in the preceding quote was altered from the original manuscript to *"the path"* in the current editions of the AA Big Book. Many of us nearly died trying to find the path, while most of us have transformed our lives by following the *directions.*

> **In my over thirty years in the program, I have *never* seen a person's life fail to improve considerably, or their joy fail to increase immensely, as a result of following this recipe precisely.**

I have seen some people fail almost exclusively as a direct result of refusing to do the difficult and sometimes even painful aspects of the program: "the self-searching, the leveling of our pride, the confession of our shortcomings, the becoming entirely honest with another human being, the making direct amends, the daily pursuit of humility and character instead of exclusively pleasure" (BB, p. 25). These consistent practices are strenuous at times (to say the least) and some days even formidable.

Yet, for those who are truly out of "bright ideas" and are willing to sincerely consider that there just might be a better way, we can earnestly assure you that if you follow the *directions precisely,* the best years of your existence lie ahead, no matter your present circumstances.

"To recover" in the context of Peoples Anonymous is simply:

to regain the great joy of living, loving, and laughing.

to once again, or maybe even for the first time, *stand in awe* of the beauty within us and in all those around us.

to feel our connection with all of life.

to discover—or rediscover—our true purpose.

to be in alignment with the Universe.

to fully embrace our authentic self and live from that place 100 percent of the time.

Over the years, prior to getting sober, I had continued to pray what we call the Alcoholic National Anthem:

"Dear God,

If You would please get me out of this, I promise I will never do it again."

In retrospect, I am clear this prayer came from a place of desperation and at times even great faith, though this plea never satisfied the *conditions for healing.* The next day, often to my own bewilderment, and always to the disappointment of those around me, I would drink again.

I learned the hard way that Spirit does for us what it can do *through* us. I kept doing the same thing over and over again, while being delusional by expecting different results. Step Two is where we start seeing and doing things differently. While we still sometimes make mistakes, at least they're not the same mistakes committed over and over again. Even making *new* mistakes might be considered progress.

In the recovery process, from *whatever* we may be healing, we sometimes speak of coming to believe as our *Second-Step experience.*

We first "come" by merely showing up—to a meeting place, a counselor's office, a church, or a spiritual gathering.

Secondly we "come to," as our Spirit within begins to awaken.

Finally, we "come to believe." This entails the releasing of *old ideas* and the embracing of beliefs that we can *authentically believe.*

I would love to be able to write this book without getting into those controversial concepts, such as politics and religion, that because of their very nature can sometimes incite great prejudice. Just the word *God* can cause some to slam their minds shut, others to fall to their knees in reverence, and still others to relive the pain of being beaten into shameful submission by the teachings of some guilt-based theologies.

Fortunately, all we need to begin the healing process is honesty, open-mindedness, and willingness. To be ruthlessly honest with oneself, to be open-minded to new ideas and possibilities, and to become willing to see things differently is *how* we begin. As a bonus, while we are in the presence of like-minded souls, we also begin to *come to* our senses.

One of our greatest awakenings here on planet earth may merely be the return of *common sense.*

What *we* mean by common sense is the ability to recognize something that genuinely fits or is of sound practical intelligence. Most rigid political stances and harsh fundamental religious teachings could not pass a "common sense" test. For example, there are those who may wonder why God himself hasn't sued most preachers for slander in light of some of the atrocious things they have said about Him.

Another interesting note along the *I never noticed that* lines appears in Genesis 2, verses 2–22: it says that God caused man to fall into a deep sleep, during which God removed a rib to make woman.

But nowhere does it say that *man* woke up.

When we received the spiritual awakening of the Twelfth Step, some of us actually felt as if we had been *walking in our sleep* all of our lives. We had been experiencing some really bad dreams, while honestly believing we were awake.

Once awake, we discover the power of following *Good Orderly Directions*. Some of us eventually begin to refer to this Power as God.

In 1935, when this technology first came through him, Bill W. needed great faith to practice these spiritual principles in all his affairs. Fortunately, today, we are in a much different place. While faith may be, according to Hebrews 11:1, "the belief in things hoped for, and the evidence of things unseen," we of Peoples Anonymous have clear evidence all around us.

In the early days, there were only a few demonstrations of the healing power of these Twelve Steps and *much faith* was required, but today, with our own eyes, we can witness the transformation of countless, previously hopeless, people from all over the world in the various Twelve-Step groups. Literally millions who were once lost are currently living happy, joyous, and free lives. So we ask ourselves:

If it can work so powerfully for so many, do I believe, or am I even willing to believe, that it can work for me? If I follow the same recipe, will I get the same results?

The only requirement to get through the hoop of the Second Step is to be willing to believe—or even to be willing to be willing to believe—in a Power greater than ourselves that can and will restore our lives to sanity, balance, and bliss if we will simply follow the recipe *precisely*. We become grateful to see this *power* initially as the power at work in the lives of others who have taken these steps. It may be the same power we have felt in the meetings, or the power we have witnessed in the life of a sponsor or the lives of friends who have recovered.

> **One of the greatest gifts ever given to the human race by this movement is the knowledge that here, in PA, you can truly have a *God of your own understanding* or even your *misunderstanding*.**

We concern ourselves not so much with what you believe as with what you are willing do in order to recover. You will know, *by your feet*, when you have honestly taken your Second Step, for they will be briskly walking you through the rest of the steps.

Step Two Exercises

1. List areas of your life in which you have *insanely* repeated the same behaviors over and over again while expecting different results. These could include relationships, finances, family, children, work, or even service/helping others.

2. Describe in detail how this actually worked out.

3. Note areas of your life that are out of balance.

4. Make a short list of *powers greater than yourself* that might be helpful in healing your life. They might be composed of the Twelve Steps, spiritual gatherings, Twelve-Step meetings, counselors, sponsors, personal principles, or a Higher Power.

5. Note the level of commitment, honor, and daily devotion you are dedicating to those things in which you believe.

6. Observe problems in your life that you have tried to solve with the same mindset that may have helped create them.

Write your personal declaration of your full intention to work the rest of these steps and to practice the forthcoming principles in all of your affairs. This is a mission statement for your new life.

CHAPTER 3

Step Three

We made a decision to turn our will and our lives over to the care of God, as we understood Him.

What might be one of the main *differences* between you and God? God usually does not attempt to play *you*.

In the basic text of Alcoholics Anonymous, loosely referred to as the "Big Book" of recovery, the beginning chapters prepare the soil for the first two Steps. Steps One and Two are statements of fact more than they are *really* action steps (though there is a lot of fruitless action usually preceding the realization of the profound truth they hold). This *activity* is referred to as the steps working us, instead of us working them. We all show up in Peoples Anonymous with at least a partial awareness of this fact: to accomplish that which our hearts truly desire, we shall assuredly need to access a Power greater than ourselves.

Approximately halfway down the sixtieth page, the Big Book reads: "Being convinced we are at Step Three ..."

Initially, this does not appear as an inquiry, but in reality, it is asking us a vital question: "Are you convinced of all the information presented within the first sixty pages?" If so, then you are ready to look at the Third

Step. If not, you must start over at Step One to find the missing link, for we are building the foundation upon which our recovery will stand for the rest of our lives. This is the launch pad from which we will be rocketed into the fourth dimension of existence and find much heaven (BB, p. 25).

There are several chapters leading up to the Third Step, such as "Bill's Story," "There is a Solution," "We Agnostics," and the beginning of "How it Works." We must be convinced of the truths in these chapters before we can genuinely take the Third Step in its intended fashion. Therefore, now, we are going to look at these truths as they relate to us in Peoples Anonymous. We will be amazed at the similarities between dealing with alcoholism and the struggles of the human condition.

In "Bill's Story" in the Big Book, there is a factual account of how the founder of Alcoholics Anonymous was beaten by the disease of alcoholism to a place of complete and utter hopelessness. His only hope for survival at the time was to be committed to an insane asylum for the rest of his life.

There, he discovered that his "dis-ease" was physical, mental, and spiritual in nature. After countless attempts, he finally realized *he* could not fix the problem. Then, he sought help from leading experts in the field of alcoholism, at which point it was confirmed he was "an alcoholic of the hopeless variety" (BB, p. xxv). In the final stage of his addiction, he realized he was "beyond human aid" (BB, p. 24).

Fortunately, he took hold of the program of action and the spiritual principles inherent in the Twelve Steps. Initially, they were passed along to him by an old friend, Ebby Thacher, who got them from the six tenets of the Oxford Group, a Christian organization founded by American missionary Dr. Frank Buchman.

After putting into practice the spiritual principles of the steps, Bill's life began to transform before his very eyes. He went from being a penniless, nearly homeless alcoholic who stole money from his wife's slender purse to get a drink to becoming the cofounder of one of the most profound healing movements of the twentieth century.

One of the reasons why the Big Book begins with Bill's story may be that for a person to be willing to take the actions that these steps require, he or she needs a real-life demonstration that they *actually work*.

This may be the juncture where the ego kicks in and screams, "I am different! I am not an alcoholic. What does this have to do with me?"

The main thesis of this book is: If the Twelve Steps can transform the lives of millions of alcoholics, they can assuredly help the rest of us with the countless difficulties of the human condition.

If this recipe can do what it has done for Bill and countless others, it can surely heal us *normal* folk.

The greatest gift that Bill had was the *gift of desperation*. We must all find the equivalent of this gift in our own lives. Bill's life came to depend on working these steps. Had he not learned to practice these spiritual principles in all his affairs, he would most likely have died a tragic, lonely, alcoholic death. So how do *we* receive this precious gift? How do we—who are not currently facing a death sentence (us so-called "normal folk")—actually acquire this essential ingredient of willingness to go to any lengths to recover?

We get it by realizing that although we are alive, we surely may not be *really* living.

In many ways, we have been living a life of quiet desperation, searching futilely for "something" where it's not. We have rarely been able to produce the desired result in any significant situation for a substantial period of time with our self-will.

This may actually be worse than dying.

Although the pain of our present condition may be the initial motivator that moved us into this work, the joy and bliss that come from the application of these steps will also draw us like a magnet to *living* this program. It does not matter *why* we come into this work; it's *why we stay* that matters.

There has been much discussion in PA about motivation, desperation, and the willingness needed to work the Third Step. But talk is cheap. We must now be willing to *do* things that may make absolutely no sense to us at first, but we must do them anyway, even those we actively resist. This is an experiential program, not a theoretical one.

In the actual doing of the *things suggested*, we will have an experience that is so profound that the understanding of *why* we needed to do them will follow. The trap we must be mindful of is "contempt prior to investigation." As the AA Big Book observes, "It cannot fail to keep [us] in everlasting ignorance" (BB, p. 568). We must be ever mindful not to draw a conclusion about this work prior to fulfilling *all* the conditions of the *entire* recipe.

The action of the Third Step is not so much about *finding God* as it is about resigning from *playing God*—in our lives and the lives of others. In its conception, this technology was summarized as follows:

> Step One: I can't.
> Step Two: He can.
> Step Three: I think I'll let Him.

The "letting Him" aspect of the Program may be a little radical for some of us with traditional religious backgrounds. In our program, the higher power can initially be anything you can authentically believe in that is a *Power greater than yourself.* Whatever this power is, it's okay—as long as it's not *you.*

As previously stated, "We cannot solve our problems with the same thinking we used when creating them." These steps are not new ideas, but simply a resurfacing of ancient truths given to each generation to assist in the reawakening of the human soul. Until we have our awakening, we are at best *walking in our sleep.*

How many times have you tried to fix a problem with the same state of consciousness that created it?

How often have you tried to manage the unmanageable?

How many times have you tried to exert force instead of admitting your personal powerlessness?

The movement that the Third Step is suggesting is more of a shift in *our* minds than *God's.*

As stated in the step, it is a decision that only we can make: nothing but our higher Self can cause us to cease looking to our lower self for guidance. Only when we run out of our own resources do we finally become willing to plug into the Resource.

This radical shift occurs when we come to the end of our self–the dying of our ego. In its purest form, the evidence of this transition is–once again–to become willing to do things that make absolutely no sense to us until after we do them.

This may sound very simple, but to the ego, it is not!

For instance, in AA, we are told to call someone who is sober when we want to drink. That makes no sense; they don't have any alcohol. Why would we want to talk to someone who does not drink when we want to drink? Besides, our egos inform us, they will just try to talk us out of it or make us feel bad about wanting to drink in the first place.

What I continually *missed* was that the Power actually came from *following* the direction, not *before* the actual doing of the thing suggested. Thinking about it, talking about it, wanting to do it, and meditating on it were of absolutely no avail.

But when I actually made the phone call *prior* to picking up the first drink, something phenomenal happened. While dialing the number of a sober guy who I really didn't want to talk to, I felt the desire to drink diminish slightly with each digit I dialed. By the time he answered the phone, 51 percent of the merciless obsession that had overpowered me numerous times had *magically* left. I then had the power to carry the remaining 49 percent to an AA meeting and further release it.

We all have our own mental equivalent of this type of lesson that may have nothing to do with drinking, but much to do with the human condition. In healing our lives, there are always many things, initially, that we feel *unwilling* to do because they make no *sense* to us. Closer to the truth, they usually offend our egos. There are also things that we have contempt for, even though we have never honestly investigated them (much less applied them to our lives).

The ego screams:

"If I don't listen to my *self*, who will I listen to? Who can I really trust? Besides, look at all I have accomplished!"

To this voice in our heads, we offer these facts for consideration:

There is a butterfly born on a branch in Maine. It travels all the way to Mexico and then returns, landing almost on the same branch where its journey began. Also, we are told, whales born in the Indian Ocean swim halfway around the world and *somehow* return home to that same spot to give birth to their young. Salmon, on the other hand, are born upriver and travel to the ocean. Then, they fight the swift current to return upstream to spawn in their exact birthplace. And we, the so-called *superior race*, usually need a GPS just to get across town.

Aligning our minds in connection to the Third Step is like positioning an antenna for better reception.

It allows us to plug into the same guidance system that is used by butterflies, salmon, whales, and possibly even the planets to move safely through our universe. We acquire the *frequency* by applying the spiritual principles of the remaining steps.

The physical evidence that we have *worked* the Third Step is the fact that we are actually *writing* a Fourth Step. This demonstration of action is our initial attempt to uncover and release the distortions in our perception that block us from hearing the still-small voice within. Through this inventory (in the Fourth Step), we are on the way to discovering our Internal Guidance System.

We realize it may seem strange to stop listening to your "*self*" so you can start listening to your *Self*, although this is just one of the many paradoxes in Peoples Anonymous. One of the most significant is **surrender to win**.

Also, one of my personal favorites mantras (if it were a tire, it would be worn bare to the treads) is:

"I am no longer interested in my own opinion."

The vibration of this thought aligns *perfectly* with the frequency that tunes us into our highest truth. In Step Eleven, some of us begin to obtain real-time, conscious contact with this beautiful idea called God. However, there is a tremendous amount of work between the Third and Eleventh Step.

Once again, in Step Three, our first direction is to *stop playing God*. It's hard to hear from *Something* that we are unconsciously attempting to simulate.

We take action by moving from the *director's chair* to honestly seeking direction. In letting go of our old ideas, we plug into the Good Orderly Direction of the Universe, or God as we understand Him. The Big Book, prior to the Third Step Prayer, addresses in masterful detail the true nature of the problem and ultimately its solution:

> The first requirement is that we be convinced that any life run on self-will can hardly be a success. On that basis we are almost always in collision with something or somebody, even though our motives are good. Most people try to live by self-propulsion. Each person is like an actor who wants to run the whole show; is forever trying to arrange the lights, the ballet, the scenery, and the rest of the players in his own way. If his arrangements would only stay put, if only people would do as he wished, the show would be great. Everybody, including himself, would be pleased. Life would be wonderful. In trying to make these arrangements, our actor may sometimes be quite virtuous. He may be kind, considerate, patient, generous; even modest and self-sacrificing. On the other hand, he may be mean, egotistical, selfish, and dishonest.

But, as with most humans, he is more likely to have varied traits.

What usually happens? The show doesn't come off very well. He begins to think life doesn't treat him right. He decides to exert himself more. He becomes, on the next occasion, still more demanding or gracious, as the case may be. Still the play does not suit him. Admitting he may be somewhat at fault, he is sure that other people are more to blame. He becomes angry, indignant, self-pitying. What is his basic trouble? Is he not really a self-seeker even when trying to be kind? Is he not a victim of the delusion that he can wrest satisfaction and happiness out of this world if he only manages well? Is it not evident to all the rest of the players that these are the things he wants? And do not his actions make each of them wish to retaliate, snatching all they can get out of the show? Is he not, even in his best moments, a producer of confusion rather than harmony?

Our actor is self-centered, egocentric, as people call it nowadays. He is like the retired business man who lolls in the Florida sunshine in the winter, complaining of the sad state of the nation; the minister, who sighs over the sins of the twentieth century; politicians and reformers, who are sure all would be Utopia if the rest of the world would only behave; the outlaw safe cracker, who thinks society has wronged him; and, the alcoholic, who has lost all and is locked up. Whatever our protestations, are not most of us concerned with ourselves, our resentments, or our self-pity?

Selfishness—self-centeredness! That, we think, is the root of our troubles. Driven by a hundred forms of fear, self-delusion, self-seeking, and self-pity, we step on the toes of our fellows and they retaliate.

Sometimes they hurt us, seemingly without provocation, but we invariably find that at some time in the past we have made decisions based on self, which later placed us in a position to be hurt (BB, p. 60–62).

One of the main theses of this book and the foundation of our work in PA is that *alcoholics do not have an exclusive on this devastating characteristic.*

Selfishness and self–centeredness are the root cause of most of the suffering inherent in the human condition.

The Big Book continues:

We must be rid of this selfishness, we must or it kills us. God makes that possible. And there often seems no way of entirely getting rid of self without His aid. Many of us had moral and philosophical convictions galore, but we could not live up to them even though we would have liked to. Neither could we reduce our self-centeredness much by wishing or trying on our own power. We had to have God's help. This is the how and why of it. First of all, we had to quit playing God. It didn't work. Next, we decided that, hereafter, in this drama of life, God was going to be our Director. He is the Principal; we are His agents. He is the Father, and we are His children. Most good ideas are simple, and this concept was the keystone of the new and triumphant arch through which we passed to freedom.

When we *sincerely* took such a position, all sorts of remarkable things followed.

We had a new Employer. Being all-powerful, He provided what we needed *if* we kept close to Him, and performed *His* work well.

Established on such a footing we became less and less interested in ourselves, our little plans, and designs. More and more, we became interested in seeing what we could contribute to life. As we felt new power flow in, as we enjoyed peace of mind, as we discovered we could face life successfully, as we became conscious of His presence, we began to lose our fear of today, tomorrow or the hereafter. We were reborn (BB, p. 62–63).

These previous few paragraphs are direct quotes from the sacred writings of the AA Big Book that address the true nature of the problem inherent in the human condition—and the solution. It pertains not only to alcoholism but also is a major component of the overall struggle of the human race. I chose to request to reprint these paragraphs verbatim because I have never seen so much beauty and truth in such few words. The wisdom and depth of these sparse writings are unparalleled in anything I have ever encountered.

I am humbled, found out, and reconciled all in one brush with this truth.

I believe that the AA Big Book may be the essence of what is considered a Divinely-inspired text or what I have come to know as a *hand-of-God book*. It contains a vast amount of information that leads to restoration and transformation. It also illuminates in a few pages the true underlying *cause-and-effect* relationship that plays out in human affairs.

When these steps were originally written, they might have been theoretical, yet today they are experiential. They are demonstrating profound results in millions of human lives.

Let's take a moment here and look more closely at each idea to ensure we have "*thought well* before taking this Step," as instructed prior to the Third Step Prayer (BB, p. 63).

As an interesting side note, this happens to be the only place I could find where the Big Book tells me to *think*. It seems that after taking the Third Step, I am to use my mind mostly for *listening* instead of *directing*.

Please do not misunderstand the true intention of this statement; we are in no way suggesting not to utilize our brains to their fullest, putting to good use all of the brilliance given each of us. This is about beginning to allow our minds to receive Guidance in contrast to playing *dictator*.

The initial direction given in the Recipe of Transformation is presented in this way:

"The first requirement is that we be convinced that any life run on self-will can hardly be a Success" (BB, p. 60).

This powerful statement awakens us to the harsh truth. We are, at times, unable to achieve the true desires of our hearts for any significant period of time when we are operating our lives based on *self*. I once heard a relevant quote ascribed to Buddha: "Everyone seems to be consumed with self, yet there's not one."

That would explain why we must come to agreement that any life run on self-will will ultimately fail. Operating our life based on a false premise while refusing to doubt its validity—even though it's not true—will ensure disaster.

This practice of "holding on to old ideas although they may be false" must be completely abandoned to allow new ideas to be installed. This process of releasing is required to reach true healing at a causation level.

"What gets us into trouble is not what we don't know. It's what we *know for sure* that just ain't so."

–Mark Twain

So, if a life run on self-will can hardly be a *success*, then let us pause for a moment and consider the true meaning of success. Our old definition may be in need of revision as we consider that real success has nothing to do with temporarily acquiring the cravings of the ego. We know that the ego is a master of acquisition. Once it's got what it wants, *then* comes the problem. Within moments, days at most, we are no longer interested in the thing we fought so hard to capture.

In contrast, when the true desires of our hearts are manifest in our lives, the flame seems to burn forever. Our desire does not fade, and the beauty gradually increases instead of diminishing.

> *A life filled with the desires of our hearts, instead of the cravings of our egos, will be our new definition of success. Although we may not always have what we want, we will sincerely want what we have.*

Previously, in our attempt to *succeed*, many of us had spent our lives in strict accord with the ego's basic doctrine:

> ### "Seek and do not find." (T-26.VII.1:4)

We were eternally looking for things where they were not. Ruthlessly, we went after trophies that we didn't even want, insisting we knew where they could be found. They were never *really* there. This eternal, futile search was closer to the definition of *hell* than to success.

Eventually, we surrendered—through a preponderance of evidence—to the truth of the Third Step. We cannot succeed in life by forcing our way on others in a constant attempt to gratify *self*. We were given the gift of desperation through a simple idea ("there's got to be a better way"). This was the birthplace of our metamorphosis.

The text then aims straight for the jugular vein: selfishness and self-centeredness, the root of our troubles (BB, p. 62). This may be a hard pill to swallow for some of us in the beginning, especially those of us who appear quite virtuous on the surface. The degree to which we are consumed with self is initially hard to behold. We disguise it in many ways, and rarely is it understood as pure and simple *selfishness*.

Some of us appear to be in constant *activity*—helping others, taking care of everyone and looking very virtuous on the outside. Even in the midst of serving others, our underlying motives *may* still be consumed with *self*. This disturbing realization is essential to begin the healing process. For some of us, this may be the first time we see where the real problem *originates*—within ourselves.

We live in a cause-and-effect universe. There is a cause for everything that happens in our lives. The good or bad news is: We're it.

We live *at cause* in the world; we truly are Co-creators in our universe. The tendency to play victim is strong—to live *at effect* while believing everyone/everything else is the problem.

As we look deeper and become more honest, we discover that if a cheeseburger *magically* appears in our life, upon closer inspection, we realize we ordered it. At some level, *we have our part* in bringing it into our lives. Some of us are willing to take full responsibility for the *external* conditions of our lives. We are willing to be accountable for just about everything, except the one thing that *really* matters—our thoughts.

Thoughts in mind produce like kind.

It is only through an in-depth inventory, coming immediately after our Third-Step prayer, that we get down to the *true* causes and conditions. In this process, we get the opportunity to reevaluate and release the things we have mistakenly attracted into our experience. This is the beginning of real freedom.

I once heard a man say, "I may not be much, but I am all I think about."

In looking at self, manifesting in a variety of ways, we may encounter self-centered fear, one of the most destructive underlying drivers of our life. It shouts, "I'm afraid I will lose what I have—or won't get what I want." When we make decisions based on these selfish, self-centered fears, things have a tendency not to turn out so well. We place ourselves in a position to be hurt, or, as I like to say, *we find ourselves at the scene of the crime.*

So our troubles, we think, are basically of our own making (BB, p. 62).

Ultimately, all we experience in life is our self, projected outward onto the screens we call our lives.

Next, we are informed, "We are an extreme example of self-will run riot, though we usually don't think so" (BB, p. 62). I fully realize we alcoholics may *seem* to corner the market on this defect of character, yet if you look closely at your own life you may find some areas where self-will is running amok. There may be some places where it's wreaking havoc, yet you honestly don't even know that *you* are the problem.

"We must be rid of this selfishness. We must or it kills us!" (BB, p. 62).

Only God, or following the Good Orderly Directions, can relieve us of this extreme selfishness. It is in the actual *application* of the steps and applying their principles to our lives that we are given genuine freedom from the bondage of self.

We are reminded: "We had to quit playing God" (BB, p. 62).

And it even tells us why: because *it doesn't work!*

One of the beauties of this way of life is its simplicity and lack of judgment. The work originates from a beautiful position of *neutrality*. I had a sponsor who, at each juncture of the Fifth Step (sharing the details of my life), would simply ask: "Well, how did that work?"

He continued, "If it worked out well for you, I suggest you keep doing it. If not, you may want to stop."

Besides all the philosophical and moral reasons why playing God is a bad idea, the simple fact is it never seems to work out well for us or anyone else. Once again, let us consider that there might be another way. *Surrendering the management of our lives* to our Higher Power is a requirement, a spiritual condition of transformation in this program of recovery. We must refuse to allow our *egos* to continue their vain attempt to run the show.

If we persevere with the rest of the program without fully surrendering to this truth, we will encounter trouble down the road. This can take on many forms, but its most common manifestation is a failure to receive the joy and bliss this program has to offer.

So how exactly do we quit playing God in our lives and the lives of others?

Another mantra that has been extremely helpful is:

"I do not perceive my own best interests."

(W-pI.24.7:1)

If we don't know what's best for us, how could we possibly know what's good for others? No matter what our age, we shift from teacher to student. We move from being the one who is always giving directions to one who is earnestly seeking guidance.

It continues with the key: "He is the Father, and we are His Children. Most good ideas are simple, and this concept was the keystone of the new and triumphal arch through which we pass to freedom" (BB, p. 62).

I was fortunate at this stage of my development to have had a very wise, dear friend share with me a beautiful idea that I have sacredly held on to ever since.

He informed me that he *believed* that in God's eyes, *he* was God's only kid. Because of this truth, his natural inheritance was *everything*, simply because of who his Father *happened* to be. He continued, "And so are you, and each and every person on the planet, God's only child. I cannot explain this to you mathematically, but you are welcome to borrow this concept if it would be helpful."

In conclusion, he warned, "Let not your pride get hold of this information. It is not for the entitled, but for the humble—not food for the ego but healing for the spirit."

Imagine seeking nothing because everything is already yours. Your only job, to fit yourself to be of maximum service to your Creator so that He can, in good conscience, give you the kingdom. The text continues: "When we *sincerely* took such a position, all sorts of remarkable things followed" (BB, p. 63).

If you are not careful, you could breeze over this small yet vital sentence without fully grasping the golden nuggets it holds.

First, the word *sincerely* is what we call a qualifier. Qualifiers are *conditions* that the spiritual technology *requires* for its successful consummation. These can be found throughout the work. They usually occur prior to a *promise* that states what will happen *if* the conditions are fulfilled. The qualifier *sincerely* comes at a very important place along this path to recovery. It literally means that we must honestly and genuinely assume an entirely new *position* in our lives.

As I tell the guys I sponsor, "You may be able to fake sincerity with your boss, your mother, and even your wife, but you can't fake sincerity with the Universe." I believe the new position, where we are no longer the director of our lives but have turned our will and our lives over to His care, may echo the story of the Prodigal Son. It is important to note that although the story of the Prodigal Son has been attributed primarily to the Christian faith, Buddha shared a similar version with the world. It was only when the son came to himself, or, one might say, his higher Self, fully realizing the absolute destructive nature of *his will*, that he *sincerely* became interested in finding another way. In that moment, he honestly and genuinely had all of *himself* that he could stand. He could not endure one more second inside his own skin. He reached out toward his Father, finally admitting complete defeat and his *personal powerlessness* to heal his life. In that instant, his life was filled with grace, and his father began preparation for his joyful return home. The feast was prepared, the robe and slippers brought to him, and God and all of the angels rejoiced at his return. He acquired this *new position* due to his spiritual awakening, *in the pigpen.*

In that moment, all he wanted to do was come home and be of service.

If we can get *there*, we will have made great progress. Once we fulfill this condition, we receive our first promise:

"All sorts of remarkable things followed" (BB, pg. 63).

Imagine a large congregation of caterpillars sitting around discussing their desire to become better caterpillars. Several have some very bright and even plausible ideas about becoming "better worms." But it seems that one of the group is not merely interested in being a "better worm." He has tried that and failed many times before. He has employed everything under the sun, from self-help books to the *I Ching*—all promising *better wormhood*.

In his endless search, he finally attends a gathering that is utilizing something called The Twelve Steps. While at the meeting, he sees a butterfly sharing the story of starting out as a caterpillar! He listens with amazement as this former worm-like creature shares his story of metamorphosis. He is most intrigued by the actual experiences of how boundless and breathtaking the view of the butterfly is in contrast to that of a worm.

This spiritual technology is not designed to help us simply become *better people* in Peoples Anonymous. However, it is designed to cause a complete transformation of our lives. Through this work, we become an *entirely different being* from the person who began reading this book.

This type of conversion fulfills the promise of the *remarkable* things that follow. We must settle for nothing less.

Once again, this program is not about *information*; it is about transformation. We awaken to the truth that we are spiritual beings having a human experience, instead of human beings having a spiritual experience. Consequently, we get to witness this type of remarkable transformation almost every day as we take others through these Steps. One of the most beautiful things that we will ever get to witness, in this life, is the living dead being born anew. To see their wings spread with our own eyes and to watch the former worm-like creature begin to take flight are experiences not to be missed.

If the human equivalent of this exact type of *remarkable transformation* is not beginning to occur in *your* process of recovery, then you must reevaluate your level of *sincerity* in connection to your new position.

If you are struggling with your ability to surrender fully, know that you can ask God, as you understand God, for the Gift of Surrender.

We must reach as high as we can, knowing that for most of us, that may still not be high enough. Many will need *Him* to reach down the rest of the way. Some cannot surrender fully. For those, the Gift of surrender will be given if it is sincerely requested.

Once that condition is fulfilled and we have assumed our new position, "We have a new Employer" (BB, p. 63).

This is a tough one to address because its implication is extremely radical, even for me. There once was a popular movie called *The Blues Brothers* in which the brothers claim to be on a *mission from God*. It's part comedy and part drama; a dramedy, much like my previous life. When I read the sentence about having a "new Employer"—with a capital E—I wondered what it might be like to *actually* work for God. Could I be employed by the Source of all things?

Since I didn't know any living person who realistically laid claim to this position (being God's right hand man), I pondered what it might be like to be the personal assistant of multibillionaire Warren Buffett. I assumed that if I performed my duties well, I would at least be very well taken care of financially. He would have at his disposal a vast amount of resources, but they would be nothing compared to the *Resource* of all things, this *New Employer*.

I must admit, the ramifications of this idea are still hard to fathom. Once we have fully taken the Third Step, we are employed by the Source of all things. Cool job.

It continues, "Being All Powerful, He provided what we needed *if* we kept close to Him and performed *His* work *well*" (BB, p. 63).

The words *if* and *well* may be two of the most important qualifiers in this entire technology. *If* is defined as being *contingent upon*.

If we expect to have all that we need that will fit us to be of maximum service to our Employer, we must first stay close to Him. We accomplish this instruction by praying and meditating daily, regardless of whether we *believe* or not, while listening for the still-small voice within, seeking guidance and direction through our sponsors, and listening for our source to speak to us in various ways, such as in meetings —usually from the least likely person in the room.

Secondly, we encounter the word *well*.

We must perform *His* work well. I am reminded of an e-card I read once that stated: "I would much rather pray for you than actually exert energy helping you." For the record, this does not qualify as performing His work well. The word *well* means *thoroughly, carefully, and soundly; in a moral and proper manner; with justice and reason.*

We must also discern: What is *His* work?

Many of us have different types of professions that we hold very dear. Some jobs are far more enjoyable than others. Some positions may be quite virtuous and even extremely helpful to the human race. I can only imagine how incredible it must feel for the doctors and lawyers who get to spend countless hours healing and defending God's kids.

One of the powerful spiritual principles that AA has helped bring back into the forefront of our daily lives with this program is *altruism*. I am not suggesting that AA, arguably a gathering of some of the most selfish, self-centered people on the planet, has a market on this powerful spiritual principle. We may have serendipitously stumbled into it because our very lives depended upon helping others *with no thought of return*. A definition I once came across best summed up this idea of altruism: "To do something for someone without any profit motive whatsoever." This was quite a stretch for us drunks, I assure you, and it could be equally challenging for most "normal" people.

The reason we are bridging the words altruism and well is, based on our experience, we must incorporate some purely altruistic activities into our daily lives if we are to perform His work well.

One of the last directives a well-loved carpenter named Jesus gave us was: "Feed my sheep." In other words, "Take care of My Brothers and Sisters." Don't just pray for them, send them nice thoughts or just wish them well. We must actually *give* of that which we have been so freely given. "But obviously you cannot transmit something you haven't got" (BB, p. 164).

We must first demonstrate these principles in our lives and allow them to bear fruit. We must do our work so that we can do the real Work.

Initially, we may *think* we are doing all of this to help ourselves. That is only a partial truth. We may begin this work for ourselves; we will stay for others. The real Work of this program is carrying this message to others and practicing these principles in all of our affairs. By participating daily in the healing of others, our lives are actually transformed.

To perform *His* work well is to transmit this gift to others— thoroughly, carefully, and in an honest manner, with justice and reason. We must feed His kids of this Truth of Life that we have been so freely given. We must behold their innocence, not their guilt, loving them unconditionally while always inviting them to come up a little higher.

We place *all* things into the Hand that originally crafted everything, trusting that He will do those things that we could never accomplish ourselves.

In conclusion, we do our work *well*, not only because our lives and our joy depend on it but also for those yet to come.

There are millions we have yet to meet who are living lives of quiet desperation, lives nowhere near what they were Created to be.

It is hard to imagine the impact of one radically transformed life. We have had some amazing *examples* throughout human history. May *we* now begin to become a living example of the beauty and power of this program of action as we take our Third Step.

Step Three Exercises

1. Imagine that you could have a God of your own understanding. What would that actually look like? What are the attributes of this Higher Power? In a few short paragraphs, describe what you choose to believe based *on your own understanding.*

2. List areas in your life where you have tried to "play God." These are the people, places, and things you have felt most compelled to direct or control.

3. Consider praying the set-aside prayer before you move into the Third-Step prayer and the rest of this work: "Dear God, please help me set aside everything I *think* I know about You, this work, myself, and my deeply held belief system so that I might have a new experience."

4. Meditate on this piece taken from lesson 189 of *A Course in Miracles*:
   Simply do this: Be still, and lay aside all thoughts of what you are and what God is; all concepts you have learned about the world; all images you hold about yourself. Empty your mind of everything it thinks is either true or false, or good or bad, of every thought it judges worthy, and all the ideas of which it is ashamed. Hold onto nothing. Do not bring with you one thought the past has taught, nor one belief you ever learned before from anything. Forget this world, forget this course, and come with wholly empty hands unto your God. (W-pI.189.7 1–5)

5. Pray the Third-Step prayer with a trusted friend, sponsor, or minister:

God, I offer myself to Thee—to build with me and to do with me as Thou wilt. Relieve me of the bondage of self, that I may better do Thy will. Take away my difficulties, that victory over them may bear witness to those I would help of Thy Power, Thy Love and Thy Way of life. May I do Thy will always. (BB, p. 63)

CHAPTER 4

Step Four

We made a searching and fearless
moral inventory of ourselves.

"The unexamined life is not worth living." (Socrates)

At the turn of the twenty-first century, my father lived in a little A-frame cabin in the Rocky Mountains. It was a beautiful place, nestled amongst the snow-covered peaks, perfectly positioned beside the Saint Vrain River. I spent many a night detoxing on my father's couch, coming down from being as high as the snow-capped mountains captured by the frosted glass window in the gable opening. One evening, we had an extreme storm that dropped several feet of snow during the night.

Upon awakening, I discovered my little Honda Accord (with the donut tire still attached to the back wheel due to my most recent flat) literally buried in the snow. There was at least a foot of snow covering the hood of the car. I had *come to* again, strung out and sick. The obsession to use was so strong I found myself, shovel in hand, digging what was left of my peg-leg Honda out of the snow. I spent over six hours in below freezing conditions, excavating my car just so I could get down the mountain to score.

That morning, my father got a real glimpse of the gravity of my problem and the extreme grip my addiction had on me. Sometimes, he likes to joke about that day by recalling, "That was truly the hardest I've ever seen my son work."

My dad was definitely onto something.

His cabin just so happened to be on a septic system, and one day it became clogged. It took nearly two weeks for the poop truck to arrive at his remote location. You could smell the odor for miles around. I'm afraid this is a perfect metaphor for how I showed up on the scene of recovery. I was also full of shit—and you could smell me coming for miles around. Even worse, I seemed to be the only one who couldn't smell it.

The Fourth-Step inventory is the process by which we begin to get honest about the stock in trade and release the damaged goods that are beginning to cause the *odor* of our lives. We aim our magnifying mind—some of us for the very first time—in the direction of our *own* shortcomings. We create an honest list of our resentments, our fears, and our sex conduct.

Referring to our list again, putting out of our minds the wrongs of others, we resolutely looked for our own mistakes. Where had we been selfish, dishonest, self-seeking, and frightened? Though a situation had not been entirely our fault, we tried to disregard the other person involved entirely. Where were we to blame? The inventory was ours, not the other man's. We saw our faults; we listed them. We placed them before us in black and white (BB, p. 67).

For me, it was as dramatic as what happened when the poop truck backed up to my Dad's septic tank and removed *everything* that was causing the problem. We show up in Peoples Anonymous at vastly different levels; I just happened to be more gravely affected than most.

It is important for me to state here, for the record: I do not now believe that I or anyone else is *actually* full of shit. I am clear that Love creates only like itself (W-pII.11.1:2): Cows have cows, not chickens. Rose bushes grow roses, not dandelions.

Our essence cannot be full of anything except the exact same Substance from which it was created.

However, we must, at times, remove the accumulated debris that covers the Light if we are to rediscover the magnificence within.

In this inventory process, we must first look at what we *appear* to have become—the parts of us that seem to have mutated—in order to unleash our Great Truth. One of the gifts this movement has given the human race is the ability to simplify the process of transformation. In the spirit of this simplicity, we are asked in the beginning of our resentment inventory one simple question:

"Who are you angry with?"

This is the heading for the first column in our four-column inventory.

This is ironic, because for us alcoholics, it is far too easy a question to answer. Simply step into any seedy, windowless, darkened bar, walk up to the man sitting on his stool around 11:00 a.m., pull up a chair next to him, order a couple of beers and inquire, "Who are you pissed off at?"

You will get an earful! If you were to help him write down that long list of well-nourished resentments, he would be halfway through his Fourth Step, if he ever made it to AA.

One fundamental premise of this book is that alcoholics surely don't have a market on anger, resentment or any other neurosis, for that matter. All of us can profit from a good personal housecleaning. Our basic text informs us, "A life which includes deep resentment leads only to futility and unhappiness. To the precise extent we permit these, do we squander the hours that might have been worth while" (BB, p. 66).

For those of us "whose hope is the maintenance and growth of a spiritual experience, this business of resentment is infinitely grave. We found that it is fatal. For when harboring such feelings, we shut ourselves off from the sunlight of the spirit" (BB, p. 66).

Today, medical researchers may have discovered a connection between holding resentments and cancer. Holding onto these unresolved negative emotions can break down the immune system and open the door to a plethora of other physical challenges. The statement that resentment could be fatal—written by Bill W. back in 1939—may turn out to be true, not just for alcoholics.

Resentment, as defined here, comes from *re-sentire* in Latin: *to feel again*. This means to re-live or replay some of the hurts of the past, done either to us or by us, that destroy the joy possible in each moment and actually cut us off from our healing.

We are told that we cannot change the past. Fortunately though, through the inventory process, we can change how we *see* the past. In seeing the past in a different light, we change our *experience* of the past. In changing our experience of the past, we gain the freedom to live fully in the present.

We find in the inventory process there are those of us who initially may consider ourselves too *spiritual* to be angry. Others have been taught that it is never okay to be upset. This type of delusion can usually fall into the category of spiritual pride and can also be released through the inventory process. Having a full range of human emotions is not the problem! It's how we channel these feelings that makes all the difference in the world. The energy once used to destroy is equally effective to create.

The initial question in the first column of our inventory was, "Who are we angry at?" This list does not only include *people*, but also principles and institutions with whom we are angry.

Actually, this is a trick question, because all we really experience in life is our *self*.

Our resentments, fears and judgments are projected upon this screen we call *our life*.

Recovery 101 introduces us to a harsh truth: "If you spot it, you got it." We can only *see* in others that which we possess within ourselves at some level. If we see the goodness in others, it is only because the goodness within us can notice it. This is equally true for the negative qualities we find so repulsive in others. If we see ugliness in the world, we will behold it in our mirror as well.

I once thought the world was full of *assholes*. Then, I realized *I* was the asshole. Nowadays, at least I'm a recovering asshole. This is a hard truth to swallow, yet once accepted, our experience of life seems to transform almost instantly. "Resentment is the number-one offender" with the capacity to cut us off from the sunlight of the Spirit and our joy: It must be the first place we look to address *the problem* at its cause (BB, p. 64).

Opposite each name in column one, we create a second column, where we write a short explanation of "What happened?" or "Why are we angry?"

Next, in column three, we look at what we believe has been *affected*. This would be the "Affects my ..." column. What *area of self* has been threatened by what we have done or what we feel was done to us?

"Was it our self-esteem, our security, our ambitions, our pride, our pocketbook, our personal or sexual relations, which had been interfered with?" (BB, p. 65).

This will be our definition of terms for *areas of self* affected that belong in our third column:

- **Self-Esteem**: How I see or feel about myself.
- **Security**: What I need to be okay.
- **Ambitions**: What I want to happen in a given situation.
- **Pride**: How I think others see or feel about me.
- **Pocketbook**: My finances.
- **Personal Relationships**: My basic ideas about how different types of relationships are supposed to be.
- **Sex Relations**: My deep-seated beliefs about how *real* men or *real* women should be.

In the third column, where we acknowledge the areas of self that have been gravely affected, we focus on one or two that have been *most devastated*. These might be considered casualties of war from a life lived on self-will.

In the fourth and final column, the field where the real power and healing begins, we start to look for our part. We remember that the inventory is our own, not the other person's. Where have *we* made "decisions based on self that have placed us in a position to be hurt" in the first place (BB, p. 62) Or, as I like to put it, where have I made decisions based on self that have placed me at the scene of the crime?

In looking for this answer, I subject each resentment to these questions:

In the entire relationship, was I selfish, dishonest, self-seeking, inconsiderate, fearful, or unkind? If so, where and how did these shortcomings set the ball rolling? We put this on paper before us in black and white. For some of us, this is the first glimpse of the true cause of our troubles. This is the vital information that we put in our fourth column, which bears the heading, "My Part?"

We must take a moment here and acknowledge that when we were young, many of us may have been innocent victims of some type of abuse. We want to make it absolutely clear in our inventory process that we *understand* that we had *NO PART* in that abuse, except for being at the wrong place at the wrong time.

Other than the times we might have been abused when we were young, as we become adults, we will usually be able to find *our part* in just about every human interaction that has gone astray. We must remember:

We are the only common denominator in all of our relationships.

This is where the program begins to invert our perception, turning everything upside down and realigning the true nature of cause and effect in our human experience. Most people live their *lives* at *effect*, falsely believing that everyone else is the *cause* of their troubles. In that reality, we are constantly trying to get other people to change, because we believe that *they* are the cause of our troubles. While living life from this erroneous position, we are trapped in someone else's reality, always believing that our happiness is dependent on *others* changing. There is always some external event that must be altered before *we* can be happy. While stuck in someone else's dream, we're lost. Until we awaken, we are walking in our sleep—and while sleepwalking, some are having really bad dreams. Living this way, at *effect*, we are busy trying to get everyone else to change so that we can get free of their nightmares.

When we move to living our life *at cause*, realizing that what we *see* in our world is the *effect* of us, the cause of the images we behold, we can get busy with our internal work and the screen we call our life changes almost automatically. We awaken to the truth that was there all along. We are the Co-creators of our world.

For some of us, this is a difficult concept. In simpler terms, take the way you see anything in your life and turn it upside down. That *may* be closer to the truth than you know.

In the inventory process, we are searching for and attempting to uncover the actual causes and conditions that are at the *root* of our problems.

So, what is the primary *cause* of the distortion in our perception? We have been operating our lives with an inverted paradigm:

We have seen our minds as victims of a screen called "life," innocently beholding the images passing by, whereas in truth, our minds are the projectors. Everything on the screen may initially come from the projector, not the other way around.

Prior to *awakening,* many of us really believed that life *happens,* and *then* we see it. This spiritual technology introduces us to the idea that the sequence is first within, *then* without. It is offering us the possibility that *everything* we see originates from our minds instead of the other way around. The problem that appears on the screen we call "our life" can usually be traced back to "us" rather than where we almost always first look, "them."

What is so powerful and so beautiful about this truth is: "us" being the true cause of our trouble *fortunately* means a spiritual awakening within "us" will not only naturally solve the problem, but also begin to heal the fundamental distortion in our perception that caused the problem in the first place.

Once our perception is healed and the way that we see things is correctly restored, this essentially begins the process of healing the *problem* that brought us to the work in the first place. This correction in our perception, when spiritually maintained, helps us ensure that we will no longer manifest as many future problems.

Although it may be hard to tell, our sincere desire is not to complicate the process of inventory. All of this is simply to help us recognize where our problems have been originating.

> *Merely beginning to look at oneself as the prime suspect in any disturbance going on around us is a tremendous advancement in the consciousness of the human race.*

Making a searching and fearless moral inventory of ourselves instead of *everyone else* is a major shift in the thinking of the world.

In its simplest terms, if you were to take a bar napkin and begin listing the things you have done that have caused harm, the shortcomings involved, and what you could have done instead, you will have made a valiant effort in the right direction of the inventory process.

After years of experience, we may have been able to improve somewhat on the bar napkin approach, but please do not lose sight of the beauty and purity of the Fourth-Step process.

We are beginning a lifetime practice of taking inventory of our own stock in trade, freely releasing damaged goods and mending that which remains on the shelf and is still of value. After we have completed our list of resentments toward ourselves and others, we begin to look at our second inventory: fear.

This inventory is where we begin to outline the things that we are afraid of. We do this in the same format as our resentment list, creating four columns. In the first column, we ask, "What am I afraid of?" As we grow efficient in the inventory process, especially when it comes to looking at our fears, we may begin to discover that they can usually be described in one of two ways:

1. **Fear of either losing something we have or not getting something we want.**
2. **Fear that we will *get* precisely what we have coming.**

We all *know* intuitively that we live in a cause-and-effect universe—that we reap what we sow. In our heart of hearts, we know what we have done or have failed to do; therefore, we live in fear of the day our actions or inactions will come into karmic fruition.

The good news of this design for living is that not only does it give us the opportunity to get honest about our fears, but fortunately, in Step Nine, it gives us a program of action to preemptively address and voluntarily clean up the wreckage of our past. This seems like the only way to genuinely lessen our valid fears. All else is smoke and mirrors.

How *free* do I want to be?

This becomes our new mantra, motivating us to dig deeper, work harder, and become even more honest and transparent with ourselves and others.

At this point, I am grateful to share my experience with what I have learned from the process of cleaning up my past. Although this is the Step Four inventory chapter, I feel compelled to spend a moment here on the idea of karma and grace.

Fortunately, my personal experience is that when I honestly and sincerely made amends in all situations in which I had been involved *and* fully committed to *never* engage in said behavior again, the phenomenon of grace flooded in as if it has been waiting there all along.

This proactive cleanup of the past suspends the natural law of cause and effect, thereby releasing the remaining consequences of those specific past actions.

As long as we remain true to that commitment to never engage in said behavior, we are truly free. *However,* if we reengage in it, not only do we reap the consequences of *that* action, we open the gate for all past karma in that area that was previously suspended by grace.

On the other hand, some fears are actually designed to give us an assignment that we must be careful not to miss. These fears are *not* based on either of the two previous ideas (losing something we have or getting what we have coming). In the fear inventory, we may discover that some of our fears are actually assignments compelling us to embrace the fear and walk through it. These could be, but are surely not limited to, living again, loving again, and laughing again. Even if we are afraid to reengage fully in some area of our life, we must. Though we may have stumbled and even fallen once or twice on the dance floor, life assuredly hopes we dance again.

Next, we begin our sex inventory. This is done in the exact fashion as our list of resentments and fears. In our first column, we write the names of those with whom we have had intimate or sexual relations and to whom we may have potentially caused harm.

We have in our second column a brief description of the interaction. Was it a casual encounter or a long-term relationship? We note the specific harm we are aware of in the second column. This column's heading is "What Happened?" Was there physical or emotional abuse, jealousy, envy, abandonment, infidelity, apathy, indifference, or emotional unavailability? Here, we write a short but detailed description of the pain caused by us during the encounter.

In our third column titled "Affects My?" we acknowledge what area of self has been most affected, just as with the previous inventories.

In our fourth column, the Power and Healing column, we ask ourselves the million-dollar question:

In the entire relationship, how were we dishonest, selfish, self-centered, fearful, prideful, inconsiderate, cruel, arrogant, or otherwise less than optimal in character?

Also in the fourth column, we ask ourselves "What should I have done instead?"

When we have completed our sex inventory, we pray and ask our Higher Power to help us mold a sane and sound sex ideal. We ask Him to help us craft a vision for our future sex life that is in accord with the *truth of our being*, not someone else's belief system.

Once we have fashioned our new idea in line with the true desire of *our* hearts, we write a detailed description of *who* we desire to attract into our lives, if we are single and desiring companionship.

Our portrait needs to be as individualized and comprehensive as possible. We shall Co-create a vision of the man or woman of our dreams. We list specific attributes, finer points and generalities we find attractive in others. We craft this vision knowing we truly deserve to be supremely happy in this life, and that usually includes a physically, mentally, and spiritually equivalent companion to share our lives.

Once the sane and sound sex ideal is before us in black and white, we metaphorically share our sketch with a wise old sage who, after listening intently to each and every brush stroke of the picture we have painted of our future soul mate, breaks out into a deep and uncontrollable belly laugh.

After he gains his composure, he removes his glasses and stares deeply in our eyes, reminding us of a great truth:

"Like attracts like."

With a kind and gentle grin, he summons us with all the majesty of a king, prescribing, "Go and become the things you have written." Then he adds, "Since like attracts like, as you become that which you desire, in a most unexpected hour, as you go about your Father's business, the one whom your heart desires shall be standing right before you."

These are the precise directions that I followed in this stage of my recovery, except when I shared my list with my sponsor, after he quit laughing, he simply asked me, "What would a woman like this want to do with a guy like you?"

He was not being mean or overly sarcastic; he was merely loving me enough to tell me the truth: if this were the quality of person I desired to attract to my life, there was much work to do! It is with great joy I can share with you that as I launched off on a vigorous course of action to *become* the prestigious attributes I had drafted, and seemingly a millennium before I made any real progress, while on the way to help one of God's kids, there she stood, and she stands by me still.

So let's go to work.

Resentment Inventory

I'm angry at?	Cause (what happened?)	Affects my? (p. 47)	My part?
Example			
1. Ex-wife: Jane	She left me, was not a good mom, treated me bad	Self-esteem Sex relations Security	Inconsiderate Dishonest Selfish
2.			
3. Employer: Jack	Fired me	Ambitions Security	Fearful Inconsiderate Lazy
4.			
5. Political system	Letting the country down, they're only out for themselves	Security Ambitions Pocketbook	Inconsiderate Dishonest/self ? Judgmental
6.			
7. Parents	Were not there when I needed them/ always working	Security Self Esteem	Dishonest Selfish

Sex Inventory

My sex conduct hurt?	Cause (what happened?)	Affects my? (p. 47)	My part?
1.			
2.			
3.			
4.			
5.			
6.			
7.			

Fear Inventory

I'm afraid of?	Cause (what happened?)	Affects my? (p. 47)	My part?
1.			
2.			
3.			
4.			
5.			
6.			
7.			

CHAPTER 5

Step Five

*We admitted to God, to ourselves, and to another
human being the exact nature of our wrongs.*

Now it's time to "take out the trash," to remove and release the things we have held onto that have been blocking us from the sunlight of the Spirit and ultimately separating us from becoming that which we were created to be.

The introduction to *a Course in Miracles* reads: "This course does not aim at teaching the meaning of Love, for that is beyond what can be taught. It does aim, however, at removing the *blocks* to the awareness of love's presence, which is our natural inheritance" (T-In.1:6).

I believe these words best represent the true movement that occurs with practicing of the Fifth Step. It is ultimately designed to heal the disease and remove the debris that blocks our awareness of Spirit's presence, thereby releasing the natural flow of love through our *authentic* self for all of life, *including ourselves*.

Deep within each of us lies our own Spiritual Truth, our essence, that which was created by God. The general consensus of most of the great mystics is: "That which was actually created by God cannot be changed by man." For the record, this was some of the best news I had ever heard. I was very grateful to consider my creator was smart enough not to entrust *me* with something that I could screw up. It also helped me believe that He knew me pretty well.

"Deep down in every man, woman and child is the fundamental idea of God," or at least the Divine Spark of that idea (BB, p. 55). The Fifth Step begins by helping us remove the blocks that have detached us from the simple and beautiful thought of a Loving Creator with whom we may have an intimate relationship.

Our directions, at this point, instruct us: "We must be entirely honest with somebody if we expect to live long or happily in this world" (BB, p. 73).

In our experience, simply getting honest with ourselves about our past does not meet the requirements to produce the needed humility that will cause the vital shift in consciousness this step facilitates. We have to talk to another human being.

We must bring into the light our deepest, darkest secrets.

We must unearth the things we swore we would never allow to see the light of day.

Only when we become willing to admit to, seek forgiveness, and make amends for the things that have been blocking us from the sunlight of Spirit can we begin to receive any *genuine* relief. It is in this moment that we begin to discover the truth that actually sets us free.

Though the concept of *telling on yourself* may be in direct opposition with everything we have been taught, and the idea of sharing such secrets might even be considered in bad taste, we cannot shrink from this occasion. In our daily encounters, and even with some close friends, such transparency may not be appropriate, but in the process of transforming our lives, this level of honesty with a trusted person—and our Higher Power—is essential.

One of the many things I find so intriguing about AA meetings is that, if you listen closely, you will hear people speaking openly in a crowd of apparent strangers about things that most people have not had the courage to be honest with themselves about, much less anyone else.

The beauty of this phenomenon is breathtaking. There have been times it has almost brought me to tears just listening to someone speak so candidly about the depth of his or her personal struggle, with no blame for others or inordinate self-loathing—just pure, unadulterated rigorous honesty.

Fortunately, this step is not asking us to walk into a room of complete strangers and bare all. It does, however, require us to find *someone* with whom we can share our life story: someone we can trust absolutely who will be completely unaffected by the information. This means we do not share our Fifth Step with anyone who would be harmed by the information disclosed.

It is imperative that this person understands that everything shared during the Fifth Step is to be kept in utter confidence, *never* to be spoken of to another person.

Only under extreme circumstances, with strict permission from the sharer, can the receiver of a Fifth Step seek outside help or reveal any contents of the conversation.

Sometimes the person we choose to hear our Fifth Step is willing to share some of his or her own deep, dark secrets with us before we begin. This may help us feel more comfortable revealing our *stuff* that we swore we'd never tell another soul about. There is something mystical that occurs when any two gather, inviting a Third, with the *intention* of bringing into the light that which has been held in the dark.

I believe this aspect of recovery was borrowed from Catholicism, in which the art of confession has been practiced for centuries. If no suitable person or closed-mouthed friend comes to mind to hear our story, a priest is usually willing and able to listen to a Fifth Step. Seasoned priests have probably heard several, for AA members have already initiated them with this Fifth-Step process long ago, and they understand the vital conditions underlying the receiving of a Fifth Step. Priests are no strangers to this recovery program; we have gone to them many times on our life-and-death errand, informing them that without fulfilling this sacred direction, we would not get over drinking, and for us, that meant certain death.

For the people of Peoples Anonymous, however, failure to follow this direction could cost them the invaluable *spiritual awakening* this process offers. Having the courage to reach this level of honesty with another human being and God introduces us to great freedom, joy, bliss, and happiness. This comes *only* through the release of all things blocking us from the light.

As Peoples Anonymous spreads worldwide, our hope is that as the steps are practiced in hundreds of groups, there will be many available for sponsorship who have worked *all* of the program. These individuals, who are willing to help others through the steps, are considered *sponsors* and are also great candidates for listening to the Fifth Step.

It is important to note that *all are welcome* at an open AA meeting. An open meeting of Alcoholics Anonymous welcomes anyone who is interested in the recovery process or simply would like to find out more about alcoholism. One *could* find a sponsor at an open AA meeting to temporarily help with the steps until the movement of Peoples Anonymous has fully blossomed.

This reminds me of a funny story I recall from a circuit speaker at an AA convention in Canada.

About halfway through sharing his life story with the crowd, he asked, "Does there *happen* to be anyone here for their very first meeting?"

He proceeded to inform the group, "Some of us have spent time in actual insane asylums. We have been bankrupt and divorced many times, and there are those of us who have been homeless, penniless, and even some of us who've spent time in Mexican jails and prisons. *We are here to guide you in your new life.*"

As a disclaimer, you may want to be a little *careful* choosing someone to walk you through this work, but you will be amazed through whom the voice of God can speak. There will be many eager to help those who are new to the program, for we all keep what we have by giving it away.

We believe that even though the average person may not be under the *lash of alcoholism* and the resulting death sentence that drives some of us to this degree of transparency, it is still equally imperative for all.

To live without the freedom and happiness inherent in completing the Fifth Step might be considered never to have lived fully in the first place. We surely do not have the market on this type of illumination; nor do we believe that we are the only ones who have ever discovered the secret of "no secrets."

There are probably millions living this way instinctively. It's just that some of us have become blocked from this gift, and without the Fifth Step, our joy may never be fully released.

One of the Fifth Step's primary intentions is to *remove the blocks* to our awareness of Love's presence.

Conceivably, becoming entirely honest and transparent with another human being could begin to clear us, allowing a deeper and more significant level of communion with the great outpouring of Love that constantly surrounds us. How amazing would it be if we could truly begin to hear the cries for help behind the crime? What if we could accept the Love that is being offered us, from *all of life*? What if we could hear the voice of our Source, loud and clear?

We find someone whom we can trust, and we prepare for a long talk.

"We pocket our pride and go to it, illuminating every twist of character, every dark cranny of the past. Once we have taken this Step, withholding nothing, we are delighted. We can look the world in the eye. We can be alone at perfect peace and ease. Our fears fall from us. We begin to feel the nearness of our Creator. We may have had certain spiritual beliefs, but now we begin to have a spiritual experience" (BB, p. 75).

The moment we have finished sharing our personal inventory with another human being and our Creator, we are to go straight home or to a solitary place where we can be quiet for an hour. We do not pass go. We do not collect $200. We do not talk on our phones or make any contact with *anyone* from the instant we complete our sharing until after we have spent this hour of Power alone with our Creator. This is essential, for if we deviate from this direction, it could cost us the spiritual experience inherent in the Fifth Step.

This may be one of the great mistakes being made in the current recovery movement. Though not intentionally, many fail to follow this direction of our recipe precisely; we are instructed to move from our Fifth-Step experience *directly* to our quiet time with our Creator.

Some who had completed the sharing of the Fourth-Step inventory had to get to work, catch up on calls, go to a meeting, etc. They seemed to have missed the mark. We must take our brokenness, our desperation, our shortcomings, and our newfound humility directly to our Source after completing our Fifth Step with another human being. Only armed with this degree of raw anguish and sorrow are we able to cry out with the plea of a drowning man for the removal of our defects of character and hopefully receive a real shift in our perception of things.

Plan ahead for this vital time with your Creator.

Do not schedule a Fifth Step until you have sufficient time to not only share your written inventory (approximately one to three hours under normal conditions) but also to spend at least one solid hour to reflect on your work *alone* with your Higher Power.

The first part of my hour alone was spent praying, *God, if you're there, please take me home, or take this selfishness and self-centeredness. I cannot stand what I have become anymore.*

My gift of desperation had come full circle. When I was first trying to get sober, I had pled with God to remove the overwhelming desire to drink. Now, I found myself beseeching Him to remove the shortcomings I was drinking to medicate in the first place: *the pain of being me,* a completely self-absorbed, self-centered, self-seeking human being. Simply put, I had lived too many years in the bondage of self.

I realize fully that we, in Peoples Anonymous, speak extensively of selfishness and self-centeredness. We have found that when all the dust settles and we have cut through the psychobabble, selfishness is the primary root of the trouble. From this malignant defect of character stem all forms of spiritual dis-ease. I personally believe it is the cause of almost all of the struggles inherent in the human condition, from divorce to war.

Even though we speak openly of this destructive attribute in the recovery process, many of us, myself definitely included, had an extremely hard time coming to grips with the depth of it in the beginning.

It was "an evil and corroding thread. The fabric of our existence was shot through with it" (BB, p. 67). We had great difficulty admitting openly that the majority of our actions and inactions were ultimately rooted in some form of selfishness or self-centeredness.

Some of us, quite unconsciously at times, became adept at hiding a bad motive behind a good one.

Only when we remove all the debris and uncover the true nature of the problem are we able to make peace with our initial internal motivations and begin to build the foundation of our lives on a higher purpose than self.

It is hard to find the solution to a problem we have not even admitted we have. We alcoholics thought alcohol was cunning, baffling, powerful, and patient. We discovered that selfishness, the actual root of our trouble, was also cunning, baffling, powerful, elusive, and quite sneaky.

I HAD BEEN LOOKING FOR THE PROBLEM WITH THE PROBLEM

It was not until I did a *thorough* Fourth-Step inventory and a rigorously honest Fifth Step that I got in touch with the depth of my own depravity.

Prior to looking honestly at the *stock in trade* of my life, I considered myself a quite generous and giving person, and, of course, when things did not go my way, I was a victim of the circumstances that had *somehow* befallen me. One of the many things I discovered was, at least with me, there was always an ulterior motive.

ℐ was a self-seeker even when trying to be kind.

It is usually darkest before the dawn, and as difficult as it may be to encounter some of these harsh truths about ourselves, the moment we bring them into the light, they lose most of their destructive power. We launch off on a vigorous course of action; when the student is ready, the teacher will appear. The moment we have found the person we can trust, we do not hesitate to schedule an appropriate time for our Fifth Step. For many of us, this may be the very first time in our lives we have ever gotten entirely honest with God, ourselves, and another human being.

Step Five Exercises

1. Meditate on anyone you may know who would be a good candidate to hear your Fifth Step.

2. This must be a person who will be completely unaffected by the information you will be sharing.

3. This must be a person whom you absolutely trust to keep your entire story in confidence.

4. This **cannot** be a husband, wife, boyfriend, or girlfriend.

5. Sometimes, a qualified complete stranger (e.g. a priest, minister, rabbi or sponsor) turns out to be best.

6. Most importantly, *leave nothing out*. Bring *all* things into the light, especially those you swore you would never allow to see the light of day.

7. Schedule a time with your "listener" and prepare for a long talk.

8. Do not try to save your ass and your face at the same time.

9. Pick one.

CHAPTER 6

Step Six

*We were entirely ready to have God
remove all these defects of character.*

In *A Course in Miracles*, there is a lesson that is repeated often:

"I am as God Created me."

(W-pI.110.6:1)

It seems that the movement in both Steps Six and Seven, for they are intrinsically connected, is ultimately toward the realization of *this* beautiful idea.

I remember the first time I heard this lesson, everything inside me screamed, *Bull___ That cannot be true!*

I knew I was a lot of things, but exactly as God created me was surely not one of them.

It was only as I began introducing new ideas into my consciousness that I started to discover, the hard way I assure you, that *everything inside me that was unlike the new idea had to come out.*

For instance, if we encounter real and genuine love, everything inside of us that is unlike that love must be released.

I am fortunate to say that I stumbled across real love. But there was a lot of "stuff" inside of me that was unlike that beautiful gift. This process is akin to a campfire: as the log burns, everything unlike the fire crackles and pops until it becomes *like the flame.* Love was one of the flames that helped transform my life, and everything inside of me unlike that flame crackled and popped until it was released. This was very hard on those around me, especially the one attempting to love me.

This process is (usually) similar to throwing up!

Most people I know are not fond of this expulsion process, nor are the ones closest to them very happy about getting inconvenienced by someone else's nausea.

> **When we make a commitment to walk the spiritual path, to release old ideas and to embrace a radical new point of view, sometimes it gets a little messy.**

Few are gifted with someone who has enough genuine care and concern to stand by them and endure this necessary process in its entirety. We release all things in us unlike the new idea we are trying to introduce, so that we can experience the Truth of our being.

Step Six is our advance in this *direction*:

To fully realize that we are now, always have been, and always will be exactly as God created us sums up the entire process of recovery perfectly. To release the barnacles we have acquired along the way, to lose interest in our attachments to (and agreements with) the dark side, and to commit fully to the light; these are the true intentions of Step Six.

Intuitively, we all know the truth about ourselves and even about all of humanity. Recovering that truth can sometimes be a challenge.

At the same time, in the healing process we aim for many perfect and beautiful ideas for ourselves and each other. Fortunately, we do this *absolutely knowing* that we are striving for progress, not perfection.

Step Six creates a shift in consciousness by which we begin to actively work to allow God to remove from us everything unlike our highest truth. In this healing surgery, where we may have thought something is being taken away, we will find a gift being bestowed upon us.

It is a spiritual exercise in values. We are simply learning: What *is* truly of value?

By letting go of things we have held as valuable, we usually discover that they are actually valueless, and the things we might have thought of as worthless sometimes wind up being of the utmost value. This is masterfully detailed in a Course in Miracles section titled "Development of Trust" (M-4.A).

In the transformation process, we notice an interesting *internal* rearrangement: we begin to grow ashamed of things we used to be proud of, and we actually become proud of some of the things we were ashamed of. Prior to our spiritual awakening, while we were walking in our sleep, we could rarely differentiate the true from the false in such matters.

Sacredly held ideas, which we were once so fond of in ourselves and others, turn out to be about as effective in the light as shark fins would be on dry land.

At this point, continuing the attempt to rearrange the seats on the Titanic by using self to fix self is no longer of interest to us. Many of us have already spent *years* trying to change, to become a *better* person. For the record, this never worked for me—not even a little bit.

I failed miserably. I gave up.

My job now is to trust the process, clean house, and help others. In Step Three, I have placed my life *unreservedly* in the hands of my Higher Power. My Creator is the One now in charge of what I am to become (and coincidentally, is a lot better at Creation than I am). This realization—getting out of the self-improvement business—is a powerful beginning of our recovery process. Fortunately, we now fully understand that we do not recognize our own best interests. This helps us to surrender the cultivating process of our lives to the Master Pruner wholeheartedly.

I once heard a beautiful story of a sweet grandfather who happened to be a master cabinet builder. One day, his grandson came to him and said, "Papa, I want to help you make a cabinet." The wise grandfather gave him a few blocks of wood, a couple nails, and a small hammer to occupy his hands. At the end of the day, *they* had built a beautiful set of cabinets. I personally believe that the grandfather was very wise to give the grandson something to hold, something to do with his *hands*, so that he could genuinely feel he participated fully in the process.

When I first heard this story, it reminded me of the Twelve Steps. It seems that the Master Healer has given us something to do with our hands, while He ultimately rebuilds our lives.

We take what we have discovered in our inventory, as well as the insights from our Hour of Power in the Fifth Step, and place them in the hands of the Master Craftsman in Steps Six and Seven. We trust that though we may not have been able to discern the valuable from the valueless, nor the true from the false at times, there is One who does, and with all the desperation of a drowning man and the humility of the newly broken, we approach the Throne of Grace.

Step Six Exercises

1. Make a list of the defects of character you have found most glaring and troublesome from your Fourth-Step inventory (dishonesty, selfishness, inconsiderateness, self-centeredness, being controlling, being self-righteousness, pride, fearfulness, greed, sloth, procrastination, grandiosity, impatience, and rage, etc).

2. List the opposite of each shortcoming: the positive attribute that would be its counterpart (e.g. prideful/humble, dishonest/truthful, selfish/selfless, fearful/courageous, inconsiderate/thoughtful).

3. Meditate on the contrast of your life: the distance between *who you were Created to be* and what your life has become. Is there work to do?

4. Ask your Higher Power daily to help you put into practice the virtues you honestly feel are in accord with the Truth of your Being.

5. Know that you don't know. (This simply means that the Creator has full rein as to the finished product: Some things will be removed, others altered, some replaced, a few left completely untouched. Our New Employer will be able to put *all that remains* into service, even though this may be extremely difficult to comprehend at first).

6. **Do not try to fix yourself.** Contrary to popular belief, this is not a self-help program. We highly recommend you not try to solve a problem with the same mind that created it. Our work is to simply prepare the soil through working the Twelve Steps and then allow the Master Gardener to bring our lives into Divine Fruition.

CHAPTER 7

Step Seven

We humbly asked Him to remove our shortcomings.

"We don't see things as they are, we see them as we are." — Anaïs Nin

While it is true that a significant piece of the Seventh Step has already begun in our "Hour of Power" with God after our Fifth Step, the spiritual discipline of this step is a lifelong journey. We have begun to reach a degree of self-honesty that we may have never reached before. Hopefully, we have looked without prejudice upon the written pages of our inventory, fully realizing that *self*, manifested in a variety of ways, ultimately caused our demise.

And hopefully, even though we have broken many hearts along the way, the final breaking of our own hearts—as the direct result of the pain we have caused ourselves and others—has brought us the necessary humility to fully embrace Step Seven.

It is with this profound brokenness and the resulting unconditional surrender that we cry out to our Creator for relief from our shortcomings—or sins, if you wish—in Step Seven.

Although our experience demonstrates that this is a lifelong endeavor, and while most of us received some real and genuine relief in our quiet time, we surely did not leave white as snow. As a matter of fact, thus far, we may have only received a glimpse into the true nature of the underlying cause of our trouble.

There once was a farmer who spent most of his days plowing the fields with an old, cantankerous Clydesdale. One day, he just happened to be tilling the soil near the main dirt road that ran through town at the southern exposure of his land. A stranger was walking along the roadside and happened to wave at the farmer. He also noticed a giant horsefly aggravating the living daylights out of the horse's nose. He could tell the ol' four-legged horse was quite distressed by his small, winged adversary, yet he was unable to shake him with jerks of his head or swats from his long tail. Out of an act of mistaken compassion, the stranger deviated from his course and entered the farmer's field. He approached the plow with the intention to swat and kill the fly. The farmer suddenly realized the stranger's plan and yelled, "Don't you dare kill that fly! Without the aggravation of that fly, this horse wouldn't move at all."

There is great wisdom in this story in relation to what genuinely occurs in the Seventh-Step process. Many of the things that I would've initially deemed needing removal as I began this process of recovery have become some of my greatest blessings. Like the Clydesdale, without them, this ol' horse wouldn't move at all.

It's interesting: though I haven't had a drink in many years, without the shortcomings that drive me, moving me farther and farther into the direction of the Light, I could easily become complacent. As I continue to walk this path, I find that the things that aggravate me most about myself compel me to do the greatest work. It seems my Employer has a beautiful way of utilizing some of my most troublesome defects of character.

In relation to the Seventh Step, all I know today is *I don't know*. Coincidentally, it appears my Employer has me on a need-to-know basis, and there does not seem to be much He thinks I need to know. There are only a few things *I need to do* on a daily basis: they are the practicing of these spiritual principles in all my affairs, combined with the habit of genuinely leaving the rest up to him.

So, in Step Seven, we take to our Creator *all* that we have discovered as objectionable.

We humbly cry out, "Please relieve me of the bondage of self."

We openly and honestly surrender our shortcomings— and that, my friends, is where we end and He begins.

We pray our Seventh-Step prayer:

> My Creator, I am now willing that you should have all of me, good and bad. I pray that You now remove from me every single defect of character that stands in the way of my usefulness to You and my fellows. Grant me strength as I go out from here to do your bidding. Amen. (BB, p.76).

The wisdom we discover in this simple yet powerful prayer, and in our story of the farmer, is that we sincerely do not know what should be removed and what needs to remain. This is precisely what we call *unconditional surrender* to the Source of All Knowing, or, one might simply say, trusting that *Father knows best*.

Fortunately, the Seventh Step clearly indicates, "We humbly asked *God*" to remove our shortcomings—not our therapists, our husbands or wives, not our mothers or fathers, not our friends, and not even our gurus, sensei, or ministers.

Many of us have sought relief from *self* through many of these methods and found them wanting. It was only when we turned in *all things* to the Father of Lights that we found real and genuine relief from the bondage of self. Then and only then did we behold a small, yet reassuring, light at the end of the tunnel.

Yet, there is action and more action. Faith without work is dead.

Step Seven Exercises

1. Find a place and time to be quiet and alone for a while and sincerely pray the Seventh-Step prayer.

2. Spend some time meditating on the prayer of St. Francis:

Lord, make me an instrument of Thy peace;
where there is hatred, let me sow love;
where there is injury, pardon;
where there is doubt, faith;
where there is despair, hope;
where there is darkness, light;
and where there is sadness, joy.

O Divine Master,
grant that I may not so much seek to be consoled as to console;
to be understood, as to understand;
to be loved, as to love;
for it is in giving that we receive,
it is in pardoning that we are pardoned,
and it is in dying that we are born to eternal life.

3. Resign from the self-improvement, self-help, self-etc. latest in-vogue movement (realizing no real and permanent transformation has ever occurred through *self* trying to change self).

4. Through practicing the spiritual principles of the Twelve Steps and by witnessing the countless lives already transformed, *trust* that when you complete the Twelve Steps and apply them to your daily life, you will become all you were created to be. (Please allow the process to unfold naturally).

5. Meditate on this illustration shared by Dr. Wayne Dyer in a lesson on "Why the Inside Matters":
    What comes out of an orange when you squeeze it? Orange juice. Why? Because that's what's in there; it doesn't matter who squeezes it. (Whatever comes out of us when life squeezes us is about us, not them). We can gauge our spiritual progress by paying close attention to what comes out of us *under pressure*.

CHAPTER 8

Step Eight

*We made a list of all persons we had harmed, and
became willing to make amends to them all.*

I n the days of the gladiators, at the commencement of battle, the
announcement rang out:

"Let the games begin."

In the Eighth and Ninth Steps, the struggle for healing truly breaks
ground and the rubber hits the road.

One of the most insightful things I've ever heard about this aspect
of our program of recovery actually came from one of my best friends,
who also has been my sponsor for many years. One day, he was sharing
with me his initial exposure to the Twelve Steps while attending his first
AA meeting. He said that during the recovery gathering, he took a quick
glance at the Twelve Steps displayed on the wall of the meeting hall.

When he got to the *God* part in the Third Step, which he intuitively
felt others had really struggled with, his experience was very different:
He actually received great comfort from the word God in the Third Step.

"I had tried to fix myself long enough," he explained. "I knew that a
higher power was going to have to be *involved* if there was to be any real

and permanent change. Besides, I used to love to drink whiskey and talk about Jesus, so I was very comfortable with the idea of God—though I was afraid that those sweet whiskey-and-Jesus days were numbered."

Then, he read on *past* the Third Step and ran across Steps Eight and Nine, which stated "made direct amends to such people wherever possible," at which point he fearfully discerned:

These people are going to want me to pay the money back!

Instantaneously, the subsequent, even more haunting thought rushed into his mind: *These people are going to want me to pay the money back to the people who don't even know I took it!*

I'm afraid he was on to something. It is true that the amends process does usually involve the squaring up of old debts—both known and unknown—by unsuspecting family members, friends, and business associates who might have been at the wrong place at the wrong time. We actually must restore those accounts to their original condition, prior to our depletion, even if we were never suspected of being the culprit.

Yet, the incredible *power* of this step lies much deeper than clearing up old debts. Let us first look at one of the beautiful opportunities this direction affords us:

The Eighth and Ninth Steps actually allow us to voluntarily clear up the wreckage of our past without forcing the Hand of the Universe to do it for us.

A lifelong friend of mine who was in her seventies at the time and just so happened to strikingly resemble the Wicked Witch of the West in the Wizard of Oz once looked me deep in the eyes, stating very gently, yet *chillingly*:

"Sonny, sometimes God whispers and sometimes he shouts. Please don't make him shout, baby!"

When the Eighth Step enters your life, you can be sure it should be considered your Universal whisper.

The Shout comes if we fail to heed our wake-up call and voluntarily launch out on a vigorous course of action to attempt to set right our wrongs. The Universe seems to have a very conspicuous way of getting our attention that usually appears in a much more taxing fashion than if we had addressed it of our own volition.

The spiritual law "We reap what we sow" has been presented to us throughout the centuries by many of the great teachers, mystics, and even a few laymen with their fair share of common sense and simple understanding of the true cause-and-effect nature of the universe.

This profound truth has been brought to us in several different forms.

In the Bible, Jesus uses a harvest metaphor:

"Reaping and sowing."

The Buddhist teaching is:

"What we send forth returns unto us."

The hippies in the late sixties had a popular mantra:

"What goes around comes around."

This inherent truth weaves through the tapestry of many different languages and belief systems, from the metaphysical idea "Thoughts in mind produce like kind" all the way to ancient convict wisdom from one of the most formidable learning centers on the planet:

"If it don't come out in the wash, it'll come out in the rinse."

Here, one might honestly conclude, with all of the press throughout the centuries informing us of this basic, fundamental law of the universe, we should perhaps be teaching the amends process in elementary school! The simple and quite obvious truth that we humans are fallible and will make many mistakes that surely require cleaning up is as elementary as the ABCs.

Somehow, I'm afraid, many of us have received quite a different message. Not only have we been convinced that a mistake is something to be *ashamed* of and hopefully keep hidden, but even more dishonest and detrimental is the delusion that we can "get away" with the harm we have caused if we somehow try to *conceal* it.

It was as if our "teachers" did not know we live in a self-cleaning universe. My personal belief is that we all intrinsically know this truth, because it was written on our hearts when we are born, though it has surely been obscured.

> *Joy,* one of the main reasons we are doing this work, *cannot return when we are daily living* with the *fear* that at any given moment, the karmic grim reaper is going to pay us a visit.

We cannot truly be happy, joyous, and free while waiting for the house of cards we built on false ideas to fall onto the floor of our glass house. There is no joy in waiting for the universe to collect the debt we know we owe because we have either refused or simply neglected to clean up the messes we've made in the past.

Steps Eight and Nine offer us one of the *greatest opportunities for freedom* known to the human race.

All real happiness is born of human relationships, whereas the birth of all pain is inherent in the pendulum of that truth. The joy in our lives resumes instantly when we sincerely admit our mistakes and offer heartfelt amends.

Therefore, our first action in Step Eight is to simply "Make the List." This does *actually* mean we get out pen and paper and start writing. This step requires, like the Fourth Step, ink on paper. This is not a philosophical or a theoretical exercise. Just like a to-do list, we need to write down the names of the things to be addressed. (The recipe clearly outlines: "We made a list of *all* the persons we had harmed").

For the record, this surely does not mean that we have to track down the name of the kid we accidently hit with a rock in kindergarten. Also, this is not a place for excessive morbid reflection; nor is it a place to superfluously beat ourselves up for all our minor, unintentional mistakes.

Rather, it is the place to bring into the light *all* of the things we *know* that we know—the things we should have and assuredly could have done differently: the people we've let down, the many misfortunes we have caused by making decisions based on self that put others in harm's way. It can be anything, from an act as naive as dating a sister's ex-boyfriend *behind* her back, to losing your temper with your child, to stealing from your parents, all the way to the atrocities that can occur in war.

Though there may be those whose names we cannot remember, we still list the harm caused in our *indirect amends* category.

As my friend and sponsor from the beginning of this chapter so insightfully shared with us, I believe we *all* already know who and what needs to go on our list. Some of us have been living with these ghosts for many years. For those of us with an acute conscience, when we are of sane and sound mind, our souls ache from the grave errors left unresolved. We inwardly rejoice the moment we realize there might be a legitimate way to transmute the past, to honestly get free and set others free, and to authentically begin anew.

Those of us with sound conscience cannot cause harm, either by omission or commission, without suffering substantial guilt. We of Peoples Anonymous are sincerely grateful for a way out of the pain of living inside our own skin.

A Course in Miracles informs us in the simplest of terms:

"Guilt is Hell." (W-pI.39.1:1)

So, in a very real and unadulterated way, Steps Eight and Nine are the keys that not only release us from the karmic debt of the past but also actually free some of us from the gates of hell here on earth, introducing us to our own personal piece of heaven.

Turning back to the first column of our list, we simply name the person, place, or institution to which we have caused harm.

Next to the name goes a short description of "the offense or injury" we feel we have caused, either by what we did or what we failed to do. In other words, we include the specific harm caused to others and/or the things we should have done that resulted in harm through our inaction (for example, failing to be the father we could have been as a result of making other choices, having other priorities, etc.). I'm sure, when we put our life under the magnifying glass and initiate a proper examination, we will find many examples of harms we have caused by failing to perform the task at hand or do the next right thing.

Socrates noted, "The unexamined life is not worth living."

This principle applies perfectly to the Fourth, Fifth, Eighth, Ninth, and Tenth Steps. Though it may be true that we cannot change the past, I assure you, we can change how we *see* the past, and that, my friends, actually changes our experience of the past and, in its own way, *changes the past*. Also, we can help others begin to see what has happened through the eyes of forgiveness instead of the dark lens of resentment.

In a real and genuine way, this correction in perception may actually *heal* our fundamental experience of life and not only change our past but also help us experience the present in a new light. When one can find innocence for the villains of the days gone by, that innocence transfers retroactively, almost instantly to oneself and somehow allows us to see the innocence that surrounds us today.

Referring back to our list, in our third column we write a very short description of what we owe or need to do to begin to make things right. This can span from a simple apology to dedicating the remainder of a life to finally being the father we could have been, the son we should have been, the sister or brother we always wanted to be, the employee or employer that is called for, or ultimately, the child of God we were always created to be.

One of my favorite lessons from the course, as previously stated in chapter 6, is: "I am as God Created me" (W-pI.110.6:1).

When I began working with this powerful idea, I am sad to report that I could find no place in my life to which I was truly showing up as I was created to be. I could find no relationship in which I could honestly say

I was showing up 100 percent, or even 80 percent, for that matter. There was no area of my life where I was not somehow blocked—and as a result, others were harmed or at minimum, deprived.

Part of my amends to others and myself was simply becoming open to the process of allowing the universe to truly have its way with me. This consisted of me *resigning* from the self-help groups *and* the Lane home-improvement seminars, thereby giving full permission to Source to bring into fruition that which I had always been created to be—that beautiful presence my heart had always longed to demonstrate in the world.

We can make three sets of lists for our Eighth Step, each respectively titled *Now, Later,* and *Never.*

On the Now list, we place the names of those in our closest circle, such as family and friends. We address our amends with the ones closest to us first, for they are the ones who may most need to be set free. They may also be the ones who will best understand *our* need to make things right and may be willing to offer us some of our best feedback, which will hopefully encourage us to continue to move forward with some of the harder ones on our list. (The actual amends process and the exact way in which we are to address each amends will be covered precisely in the next chapter on the Ninth Step).

The Now list can also hold the ones who live close to our current geographical location or people or institutions which we can easily access.

The Later list can be composed of those who live far away; there may even be some family on this list, just because of their challenge, geographically. Those on this list may require a plane ride, a cross-country drive, or at least an in-depth long-distance phone call.

Our experience has taught us that once we have completed the Now list, we will have received a sufficient amount of inner peace and real joy to motivate us to move towards the Later list. Then, once we have completed our Later list, we will be so full of bliss and will have found such freedom that we will finally be willing to address the short list of names we swore we would *never be willing to do* on our Never list.

This concludes the *making a list* portion of Step Eight. Whether you have three names written on a Post-It note or a three-subject notebook filled from front to back, we want to remind you that *you are not alone.* We encourage you, be not overwhelmed; know that the Power goes with you wherever you go. Ultimately, it is *He* that doeth the work. Our key to unlock the door to freedom is willingness. Based on our actual experience, you will be given all you need to make things right the moment you are ready to give it away, knowing it was never *truly* yours in the first place.

Step Eight Exercises

NOW

Name	Harm Caused	Amends Needed
1.		
2.		
3.		
4.		
5.		
6.		
7.		

LATER

Name	Harm Caused	Amends Needed
1.		
2.		
3.		
4.		
5.		
6.		
7.		

NEVER

Name	Harm Caused	Amends Needed
1.		
2.		
3.		
4.		
5.		
6.		
7.		

CHAPTER 9

Step Nine

*We made direct amends to such people wherever possible,
except when to do so would injure them or others.*

L et us begin with a few insightful definitions of the word *amends*:
To compensate, to alter, to modify.

To improve.

To grow, to become better by reforming oneself.

To remove or correct faults, to rectify.

One of my personal favorites, and the one that seems to come closest
to the original intention of this technology as it came through Bill, reads
as follows:

To restore to its Original condition.

When I began this aspect of the recovery process, the conditions of
my relationships were many things, but "reminiscent of their original
condition" was not one of them.

**Who among us could not benefit greatly from a spiritual
discipline that has amends as a part of its common practice?**

With this as our next direction, Step Nine launches us off on a vigorous course of action to *actually* begin cleaning up the wreckage of our past. We do our utmost to sweep "our side of the street," even though there may be those on our amends list who actually hurt us far more than we ever hurt them. We focus only on the harm *we* have caused. The actions of others, as appalling as they may be sometimes, do not let *us* off the hook from the necessity of attempting to set right *our* wrongs.

Please allow me to share the following example, taking care to mention that we *never* speak openly about the information entrusted to us in a Fifth Step by directly using the name of the person who told us their story. We can, however, share in a general way what we have learned in that process if it might be helpful to others **while strictly keeping the source in utter confidence.**

An experience occurred a few years ago that will bring this aspect of the amends process into light perfectly. One evening, I was listening to a Fifth Step at a public park somewhere deep in the hood of Miami, Florida. It was a very exhaustive piece of work and was lasting into the wee hours of the morning. While listening to the young man's in-depth sharing of the painstaking details of his life, at approximately 2:00 a.m., I honestly began thinking, *What the hell am I doing here?*

Mosquitos the size of small hummingbirds were biting my legs and ankles every ten seconds. Unfortunately, I still had on my swim trunks from a day at the beach.

I also recall thinking, by nearly 3:00 a.m., *You know, I don't really even like this guy very much. Why am I here in this park at 3:00 a.m. and not back at my condo, snuggled up with my beautiful wife and son?*

(This thought is actually an entirely different story that would speak to the question of motivation and dedication that is bred out of one's personal desperation and willingness to go to any lengths for healing).

Yet, the powerful lesson I learned from that Fifth-Step session with the young black man sitting before me came from the words of *his* mouth.

It seemed that his wife had recently had an affair, while he was on one of his long drinking binges. To hear him tell it, he would be gone for *days* drunk, expecting her to stay home and take care of the kids and somehow hold things together while he was out catting around.

When he first got sober and found out about the affair, he *understandably* became very angry. But he began to verbally abuse her, daily! She felt horrible for her actions and desperately wanted the best for him and the family, and from the moment he got sober, she ended the affair and admitted her wrongs and her willingness to set matters straight. I'm afraid this was not enough for him. He continued to rub her face in the transgression and treat her with extreme cruelty.

Upon his revealing of this ongoing behavior in his Fifth Step, I immediately informed him that he must stop treating her in this fashion, and he must make amends to *her* for the way he had treated her *after she cheated on him!*

I shall never forget the look on his face, for even though it was the dead of night in that mosquito-infested park, his face full of anger, bewilderment, and confusion perfectly resembled a deer caught in the headlights. The look was priceless. In a way, it nearly made the long hot, tiresome night worthwhile. For he genuinely asked me, quite distraught, "Do I really have to make amends to *her* for the way I treated her for cheating on me?"

What came out of my mouth surprised even *me*:

"Well, my friend, that's why they call this work."

Even though her "sins" may have been many, he *felt* his were few, declaring, "I never cheated on *her*," However, this in no way negated his need to make amends. He needed to clean up *his* side of the street, not only for his abusive reaction to her indiscretions but also for his part in abandoning her during all the drinking binges that *may* have contributed to her transgression in the first place.

I realize that this may be an extreme example of the amends process and the way in which we must address our part even though "they" may assuredly have made their own mistakes. But we must address this dichotomy out of the gate, for we may find various versions of this dynamic in radically different degrees throughout the amends process.

When we begin to make our actual amends, working from our Eighth-Step list, we schedule one or two meetings a week. Hopefully, we will have the opportunity to sit down in person with some, while others we will have to reach via teleconference as we start at the top of our list titled "Now." We call each individual first and inform them that we would like to schedule a time together, preferably in person. We initially *let them know our intention* for the meeting: We wish to "make amends for our past behavior. We are working our Ninth Step." We want to actually mention that we are involved in working the steps, for we never know when we might encounter one who may also be in need of healing through this work or someone who knows or loves someone who might be helped by it. After *we* make our amends, they may ask us if we are willing to help them or a loved one.

We are there to address the mistakes we have made and bring them into the light of day. We also want to offer the other person the opportunity to share with us *their* experience of our relationship. This is an extremely important part of the amends process that is sometimes missed. If neglected, it may cause failure of the entire process and rob us of our spiritual experience.

> **We must realize on a very sincere level that what we *thought* happened and what *really* happened may be two *entirely different* things.**

In each amends, we share our perception with the other person of what we did, and/or what we feel we should have done, while we humbly realize there may be serious distortions in the way we saw things and as a result held them in memory.

There is a beautiful lesson in a Course in Miracles:

"Forgiveness recognizes what you thought your brother did to you has not occurred" (W-pII.1.1:1).

I believe the "has not occurred" part is referencing "in God's world," for it surely *appeared* to happen in ours. This might also be considered "in Reality, capital R," instead of the world we see through the eyes of the ego. This lesson suggests that our perception of things may be distorted, and as a result of the distortions in our perception, we cannot see what's *really* happening.

Here, we uncover the truth inherent in a statement made by Jesus: "Do not judge by appearances."

Why not?

Because they are *appearances*. Our awakening will reveal to us that things are rarely as they appear.

This aspect of our spiritual awakening may also unveil the profound truth that everyone is always doing one of two things: saying either "I love you" or "Please help me."

One of the greatest gifts or curses (depending on your perspective) that is born from us becoming awake through this work is:

We begin to see the cry for help behind the crime.

(Interestingly, "crime" is an insightful word: crime = cri-me = me cry for help).

We actually begin to see the "please help me" that lies behind the "I hate you." In other words, where there is an *appearance* of a crime or offense, we begin to see the reality of the cry for help. We may discover that America's Most Wanted were actually America's Most Unwanted, but *they finally found somebody to want them.*

We truly begin to hear the calls for love behind the cries for help. (These are usually masked within the lower vibrational expressions of anger, fear, jealousy, pride, prejudice, etc.). The amends process internally heals our perception so profoundly that it actually allows us, and those to whom we've made amends, to begin to see things radically differently.

In many circumstances, we genuinely realize that neither what we *thought we did* nor what we *thought was done to us* ever actually occurred in the way we may have held onto it in our memory for all those years.

As we honestly see the cries behind the crimes, ours and the other person's, with our newfound healed perception, we find real forgiveness, true freedom, and in some rare cases, an understanding that surpasses our understanding.

In the amends process, we do not reveal specific details to others that will simply cause them harm, always employing this principle:

Honesty without compassion is cruelty.

There may be times when revealing specifics would only cause further harm; therefore, we will share about past harms in a general way.

For instance: "There are many things, _____ (name), that I did that I deeply regret, and/or there are things I deeply regret not doing that I desperately wish I would have done."

We may also include the admission of the specific defects of character that were involved in the harm caused. The following is an example:

"I deeply regret my dishonesty, my selfishness, my self-centeredness, my self-righteous pride, my cruelty, my arrogance, my inconsiderateness, etc."

Acknowledging the shortcoming in ourselves that was the underlying cause of the harm is sufficient in most cases, especially when to offer details of the specific behavior would only result in more harm. For instance, if one has had an extramarital affair, to go into great detail about the specific circumstances and to offer the name of the individual involved *could* fall into the category of causing more harm, not only to the current spouse but also to the other participant as well. *Each instance must be prayerfully considered.* We have no recommendation as to what is genuinely in the best interest of everyone in situations such as these. After extensive meditation and the seeking of guidance from a sponsor and/or trusted closed-mouthed friend as to the appropriate action to take, one *can* fulfill the conditions of the amends process by simply acknowledging the shortcomings that were involved (such as selfishness, dishonesty, inconsiderateness, etc.) and expressing the desire to make amends. We cannot save our skin at the expense of others.

At the same time, we *must* hold ourselves to a very high standard with this principle, never using it to simply get out of the humbling experience of getting honest with someone who truly deserves the whole truth, where revealing the specifics of the information would genuinely not cause greater harm.

After we have spoken to the action, inaction or shortcoming that *we* remember from the experience, we always ask the other person: "Would you please share with me *your* experience of our relationship or encounter or the things that were most hurtful to you that might be helpful for me to take an honest look at?"

We fully realize that they may have an entirely different perception of the way things happened.

Once they begin speaking, we do not interrupt, rationalize, or attempt to justify their perception or understanding of things.

If it is different than ours, or if they remember the experience in an even more negative light than we do, we simply say, "Thank you so much for sharing. I deeply regret you feel that way. What can I begin to do to make things right?"

We avoid the *highly overused and extremely undervalued* phrase "I'm sorry."

Most of us have heard "I'm sorry" enough times to last a lifetime, and the statement is fundamentally untrue, for we are not *sorry*, wretched human beings. In essence, we are all beautiful, innately innocent Children of God who have simply made some grievous errors, which we desperately wish to amend and we hopefully deeply regret. The word that may best describe the true emotion driving the amends process is *regret*: to feel remorse, a sense of loss, and deep disappointment in oneself.

When we say to someone:

> **"I deeply regret and feel very remorseful and disappointed about the things that I did or failed to do, and I desperately desire to make amends. What can I do to make things right?"**

—they get it.

This, of course, is substantially more meaningful than "I'm sorry."

Coincidentally, this may be one of the most powerful arrangements of healing words that has ever been uttered in the human experience. You will be amazed before you are halfway through this amends process, because you will discover the profound healing power of a heartfelt word shared honestly in a sincere attempt to make things right.

Referring back to our list again, there will be some amends we will not be able to make directly:

1. Some of those affected have passed away.
2. For some, making contact would honestly cause greater harm.
3. For others, our greatest amends would be to simply leave them alone.
4. There may also be those we cannot find, even in today's small world of social media.
5. We may be unable to remember some people's names, or we may not have any idea of their current locations, although we vividly remember causing person X harm.

All of these and others that qualify similarly will fall into the category of *indirect amends*. We are fortunate to have, in this spiritual technology, a way to clean up the wreckage of the past indirectly.

We will creatively find ways to make these amends. We can volunteer with Big Brothers and Sisters of America, for instance, for failing to be the sibling we should have been. We can help out with the battered women's shelter for harms caused to an ex-wife or ex-girlfriend with whom future contact would cause more harm. We can participate with Meals on Wheels to make amends for failing to be there for some elderly person in our life, such as a grandmother or grandfather.

This list can increase with your creativity and willingness to do some equivalent good for the wrongs done to those to whom we cannot make amends directly. All of the names or markers for the "no-names" will be on our Eighth-Step list.

When we have fulfilled our commitment to the chosen organization or set of individuals, that we are using to address specific indirect amends, we can mark the corresponding name off our list— *and our conscience.*

Then, there may also be those amends we are to make that actually come to us by "coincidentally" crossing our path.

The one on my list who I felt I'd caused the most pain was my sweet grandmother, Memaw. She passed away when I was eighteen years old, and I did not begin to seek recovery till I was in my twenties. She was my very best friend in the whole world.

She was my greatest teacher, my safe place, my shelter from the storm.

I'm afraid I, on the other hand, was like a tornado in her life, literally ripping through her world and leaving nothing but devastation and destruction behind.

I can honestly say I never meant to cause her harm, nor most of the others who were on my list, yet in my selfish and self-centered ways, I somehow always managed to cause harm to the ones I loved the most, especially Memaw. This literally haunted me in my early recovery.

The shame, guilt, and unrelenting remorse visited me daily.

The others on my list also deeply bothered me, yet, because Memaw had demonstrated such a great expression of unconditional love toward me in my life—and I had somehow managed to hurt her the most—this one needed immediate action.

I had absolutely no clue how to even begin to heal this.

Obviously, there was no way I could make my amends directly to her, for she had passed away many years before, and there was equally no way I could get free without addressing this issue, at least indirectly.

Then, one day, I "coincidentally" met an elderly woman named Marie.

She was approximately eighty years young when our paths crossed, a vibrant, frisky and rather wild old lady who just happened to be celebrating thirty-two years sober at the time.

I had been desperately trying to get sober for many years previous to our encounter. In the beginning of our relationship, I assure you, she helped me far more than I ever helped her.

She happened to be sharing at a recovery meeting the afternoon we met. She reminisced of the old days of working brothels, servicing the "service men," selling door-to-door encyclopedias, and eventually becoming a 911 operator for the Austin Police Department. This all came through her sweet, raspy voice along with a gleam in her eye and an unmistakable bliss in the infectious tone of her voice. I knew immediately we were cut from the same cloth; we were the same spiritual blood type. Though we were many years apart, she spoke in a language I could somehow deeply relate to, even though I'd had minimal actual experience with the "old days" of which she shared openly with us that day at our meeting.

I was only a few months sober and struggling tremendously with the whole process of recovery, especially the concept of long-term sobriety. I knew I needed to stay sober, and a part of me even wanted to be sober (long enough to get my affairs in order), but long-term sobriety dramatically resembled long-term suffering to me.

To imagine life without my medicine was quite unbearable. Alcohol was not my problem; it was actually my solution. It was the medicine I needed to treat the problem: me.

Marie was one of my first living examples of a person who had been sober for many years and displayed beauty, grace, a profound love, and a great wisdom, accompanied by compassion and *real* joy. She was genuinely happy while bordering on what appeared to me to be my first actual encounter with an elusive gift sometimes referred to as bliss.

I immediately adopted her as my new grandmother, and as she helped me in the early days of my sobriety, I was able to help her with the many mundane things that an elderly woman living alone often needed.

One day, she informed me that she wanted to return home to the place of her birth to see a few of the only surviving family members she had left on the planet and to pick up her thirty-four-year sober chip at her home AA group in Kansas City, Missouri.

I was single at the time and honestly had nothing better to do, nor anywhere else I really needed to be, so I decided to chaperone her on the trip. I must admit, it was one of the most unique experiences of my life. At first, I felt more like an "escort" than a chaperone, from some of the looks we received traveling through the airports and hotels, yet we laughed it off and were both quite well- mannered and even somewhat behaved.

We flew to her hometown, spent time with her family and friends, picked up her AA sober chip and, one evening, we managed to hit 7th & Vine St., a hot music spot deep in the hood on the bad side of town, just in time to catch some live jazz and some of the most authentic blues I've ever heard. We just so happened to be the only two white people in the entire bar. I took off to the restroom while Marie headed toward the dance floor. When I returned from the restroom, I found Marie on the dance floor, literally dancing with the lead guitarist.

In that moment, I suddenly knew we were going to be okay.

We had a blast, and most importantly she got to spend some quality time with her family and friends for what turned out to be one of the last times in her life. Within a short time of our return to Austin, I'm afraid she had a serious fall—on another dance floor, interestingly enough—and her life took an immediate turn for the worse. Marie was dancing at an AA hall on New Year's Eve, one of her favorite things to do, when she fell, but instead of breaking her hip, like many elderly folks do when they fall, she managed to hit her head. She was rushed to the emergency room only to discover that the fall had caused a hematoma (internal bleeding) in her brain, and immediate brain surgery would be necessary if there was to be any chance of her survival.

Fortunately, my wife and I were called immediately, and we rushed to the emergency room as the clock struck midnight. The doctors informed us that to attempt brain surgery at her age would probably kill her and that they believed she'd had a long and productive life. It seemed they were not too interested in doing the surgery and were subtly hinting they did not recommend the procedure.

I asked them, "What will happen if you do not do the surgery?"

They informed me that she would die before morning due to internal bleeding.

I asked, "What will happen if you do the surgery?"

I was told she would probably die.

In no uncertain terms, I directed the doctors to get to work.

We were up all night while they were performing brain surgery on an eighty-something-year-old lady. It was touch-and-go.

She surprised everyone and survived the operation.

Two weeks later, while she was still in the ICU, they discovered another small bleed, and an additional brain surgery was required.

I had been unable to be with my sweet Memaw while she was in her greatest moment of need. Due to my addiction, when she was in the hospital dying of cancer, I was in jail. However, I was able to be there daily for Marie while she went through two surgeries, a month in the ICU, several months of hospitalization, rehab, assisted living, and, ultimately, her last years of life at a nursing home with her little dog Copi by her side.

I was given the greatest gift: an opportunity to make indirect amends to Memaw by simply being present, sober, and available with my sweet friend Marie, and I was able to help her walk through one of the toughest seasons of her life.

When Marie passed, we had a little service for her at the same AA hall where she fell that dreadful New Years Eve.

She ultimately began her transition doing one of the things she loved the most: dancing.

I still deeply regret the pain I caused Memaw. I suspect that may never go away. Even though Memaw may have never held any of my mistakes against me, I did. However, helping Marie helped me get *free*, and I believe wherever they are, Marie and Memaw are now together, hopefully hanging out and doing a little dancing. It is helpful to feel we have such great souls possibly awaiting us on the other side.

> We discover that the healing process of amends may be as much or even more for us than for the other person. When we consciously, intentionally, and voluntarily launch off on a vigorous course of action to work these Steps and do all we can to clean up our side of the street, we encounter a way of living that actually brings us more joy than can any drink or drug on the planet.

Referring back to our list, we note that during our direct amends, sometimes the response we receive may be less than favorable.

This is genuinely okay. We are there to do our part. We cannot control the outcome. We must constantly remind ourselves that although we honestly desire to do all we can to set things right, there will be those situations that—or people who—for whatever reason, may not want to let us off the hook. Some people may choose to cherish and even nurture their resentments, and that is absolutely their right and none of our business.

We, on the other hand, no longer have any use for withholding forgiveness, maintaining any form of spiritual pride, or failing to release our self-righteous indignation. Fortunately, we now fully realize that resentment in all forms shuts *us* off from the sunlight of the spirit, and in that darkness, our joy and our recovery begin to wither and die.

> The amends process actually allows all things in our lives to have the opportunity to literally begin anew.

We have learned, in the trenches of this work, that no form of healing is impossible—no matter the gravity of harm caused—when the harm is honestly and humbly acknowledged and sincerely offered unreserved restoration.

If we are painstaking about this phase of our development, we will be amazed before we are half way through. We are going to know a new freedom and a new happiness. We will not regret the past nor wish to shut the door on it. We will comprehend the word serenity and we will know peace. No matter how far down the scale we have gone, we will see how our experience can benefit others. That feeling of uselessness and self-pity will disappear. We will lose interest in selfish things and gain interest in our fellows. Self-seeking will slip away. Our whole attitude and outlook upon life will change. Fear of people and of economic insecurity will leave us. We will intuitively know how to handle situations which used to baffle us. We will suddenly realize that God is doing for us what we could not do for ourselves.

Are these extravagant promises? We think not. They are being fulfilled among us—sometimes quickly, sometimes slowly. They will always materialize if we work for them. (BB, p. 83–84)

Step Nine Exercises

1. Take your Eighth-Step list, beginning with the *nows*, and make initial contact with at least two people weekly, attempting to schedule a face-to-face, in-depth conversation. (You may schedule a teleconference if they are not local and a trip to see them in person is not possible at this time).

2. Inform them *up front* the precise intention of the forthcoming meeting: That you need some of their time and attention to begin your amends process with them. Please do not catch people off guard or launch into an amends without giving them clear forewarning and ample time to prepare for this conversation.

3. Express your sincere regret for harms caused, both by commission and omission (things you did unintentionally or intentionally that caused harm or for things you failed to do that you wish you had done).

4. *Never* point out anything the other person may have done, *their* shortcomings, during *your* amends to them. Focus only on your part of the problem/fallout/controversy/harm. (No exceptions).

5. Most importantly: After you have acknowledged your mistakes in a general way, ask them to please share with you *their* experience of the past and how they felt about things. (Do not say *a word* during their sharing; do not rebut, rationalize, justify, explain, or in any way attempt to deny, alter, or undermine their experience. *Just listen.*)

6. When they have completed their sharing of what it was like for them during their encounter/relationship with you, simply ask, "What can I do to begin to make things right?"

7. Once again, *only listen*.

8. Depending on the overall conditions of the amends (e.g., each person's sincerity in his or her desire to *really* get free), the requests will usually be honest, manageable, and fair.

9. As long as it meets these conditions, do your utmost to fulfill the other person's request as quickly as possible. (With financial amends, when able, square up immediately. If needed, always possess the humility to pay back the money in modest payments).

10. For those who require a living amends: *stay the course*. For example, do not make amends for working too much, failing to be an active dad, and then turn around and neglect your child due to a new endeavor.

11. Finally, when it's done, *let it be*. (Do not look back in morbid reflection, attempting to punish yourself further for past mistakes. Use the past *only* to help others understand that you can relate/identify with their struggle and are thereby qualified to assist them in their healing).

Dos and Don'ts: Be ever mindful when making direct amends to ex-wives, ex-husbands, ex-lovers, etc. For the record, these should usually go on the Later list, if not the Never, simply because they are to be done last, not first. We must be very careful with our motives and intentions in these specific situations. When the time comes and we have done our work through the amends process and finally come to these individuals to make direct amends, we are to simply acknowledge the pain we have caused and the shortcomings involved and ask them what we can do to make it right. (Usually, we do not afford those who are still hostile toward us the opportunity to share their *experience* of our relationship, for they might use it as an opportunity for revenge).

Helpful Tips/Phraseology for the Amends Process:

- "There are many things, _____ (name), that I did that I deeply regret, and/or there are things I deeply regret not doing that I desperately wish I had done."
- "I deeply regret my dishonesty, my selfishness, my self-centeredness, my self-righteous pride, my cruelty, my arrogance, my inconsiderateness, my controlling and demanding behavior, etc."
- "Would you please share with me *your* experience of our relationship or encounter, or the things that were most hurtful to you that might be helpful for me to take a look at?"
- "Thank you so much for sharing. I deeply regret you feel that way. What can I do to begin to make things right?"
- "I deeply regret and feel very remorseful and disappointed about the things I did or failed to do, and I desperately desire to make amends. What can I do to make things right?"

CHAPTER 10

Step Ten

We continued to take personal inventory, and when we were wrong promptly admitted it.

We continue to take personal inventory and continue to set right any new mistakes as we go along. We vigorously commenced this way of living as we cleaned up the past. We have entered the world of the Spirit. Our next function is to grow in understanding and effectiveness. This is not an overnight matter. It should continue for our lifetime. Continue to watch for selfishness, dishonesty, resentment, and fear. When these crop up, we ask God at once to remove them. We discuss them with someone immediately and make amends quickly if we have harmed anyone. Then we resolutely turn our thoughts to someone we can help. Love and tolerance of others is our code (BB, p. 84).

Watch is the Keyword of the Tenth Step.

In our entire recipe of transformation, nowhere does it give *us* permission to take our eyes off of *ourselves* and aim our magnifying vision at *other people*. It consistently directs us to look toward the place where the "problem" usually originates: within ourselves. Many of us, prior to encountering the Tenth Step, had been *unconsciously* living our lives "continuing to take others' inventory, and when *they* were wrong, promptly pointing it out to them." As much *fun* as that may have been, it is a complete waste of energy. Wisdom's greatest gift is the realization that if we are to change the world, the change must come from within. Gandhi taught, "Be the change you wish to see in the world."

Yet, the spiritual axiom holds that whenever we find a flaw in *anyone*, it is merely an indication that *our* perception has become distorted and is in need of correction.

This is a hard truth to swallow, but once fully digested, its nutrients sustain a vibrant and joyful life.

Step Ten is the beginning of a *practice* of truly releasing the fundamental blocks that ultimately cause our misperceptions. First of all, throughout this entire process, we are taught to search for the flaws in our makeup that are at the root of our troubles and to *watch* for the places in our lives where we continue to make decisions based on self that place us in a position to be hurt.

Step Ten also teaches us to make spot-check daily inventories—taking a searching and fearless account of ourselves as needed. We are directed to continue to watch (be mindful of) our motives, our thought life, our actions, and our inactions. I believe one of the many reasons this technology works so beautifully is that we are no longer allowed to live our lives in the old way: taking *others'* inventory and promptly informing them of the extremely grievous error of their ways (which, for the record, seems to never produce the desired result in any situation, and instead fosters resentment).

As hard as it may be to imagine, we are incorporating a profound lifelong spiritual practice by simply beginning to watch.

We watch for dishonesty, selfishness, fear, self-centeredness, resentment, inconsiderateness, pride, ego, self-righteousness, and any other lower vibrational responses to life. When these old companions crop up, as they assuredly will, we immediately ask our Higher Power for their removal. Next, we bring them into the Light by confiding in a closed-mouthed friend or working with our sponsor. We have discovered, through this process, the inherent power of living a life of transparency with those we can trust. In the Tenth-Step inventory process, we have fortuitously discovered that defects of character regularly exposed to the Light diminish greatly over time.

As we do this, the Tenth-Step process directs us to make amends promptly if someone has been harmed and instantaneously turn our thoughts to someone we can help.

The activity of the inventory process chiefly involves *watching*, but some choose to write as well. Some journal, while others write out Tenth-Step inventories in a variety of other formats. This practice might be considered the microscope we place our shortcomings under.

The real extraction and ultimate removal of the root cause of our trouble (selfishness) comes from the gravitational pull of *service*. It is in the Tenth Step that some of us make our first genuine strides toward true altruistic service. This is a vital and essential ingredient in any transformed life: a regular practice of doing something with absolutely *no* profit motive.

When we have found the true culprits of our downfall through the continued practice of personal inventory and gained the humility needed to promptly admit them, the real journey begins. We rapidly take strategic action in the opposite direction of that defect of character and find substantial release of a lasting nature.

For example:

Practicing faith instead of fear.

Practicing honesty instead of dishonesty.

Practicing humility instead of pride.

Practicing being considerate instead of judgmental.

Practicing giving instead of taking.

Practicing thinking of others instead of ourselves.

Practicing love instead of fear.

Practicing kindness instead of retribution.

Practicing forgiveness instead of blame.

Employing these practices begins to relieve us from the bondage of self, and this can occur only as we shift our thoughts and actions toward purely altruistically helping others.

We find this principle behind all of the steps and in most aspects of the program, though in Ten, Eleven and Twelve, we boldly face the reality that a life full of joy and bliss is always built on a foundation of service. This is truly the driving force of the entire program.

To conclude our Tenth-Step discussion, let us consider what we can learn from a missile guidance system:

We are told, once launched, that the missile has absolutely no idea where it's going. It is only through a process called *negative feedback* that the missile can hit its target. When it starts to veer off course, a built-in alarm system gently moves it back in the direction of the target through a series of realignments.

Like the missile, the human life needs to get back on track sometimes. The Tenth-Step process of admitting we were wrong, seeking divine intervention for the removal of our shortcomings, making amends quickly, and immediately launching off on a vigorous course of action to help others is our new built-in guidance system. The practice of *watching* is our way of initially activating the system, while listening to *negative feedback* is what helps us stay on course. Coincidentally, by practicing these principles in all of our affairs, we seem more likely to hit the target.

This is the essence of the Tenth Step. These inventories can be taken daily, weekly, or monthly. You will find your own personal spiritual calibration and the regularity needed to grow and maintain your fittest spiritual condition.

Step Ten Exercises

(Adapted from BB, p. 86)

1. When we retire at night, we constructively review our day. Were we resentful, selfish, dishonest, or afraid?

2. Have we kept something to ourselves that should be discussed with another person at once?

3. Were we kind and loving toward all?

4. What could we have done better?

5. Were we thinking of ourselves most of the time?

6. Were we thinking of what we could do for others, of what we could pack into the stream of life?

7. We must be careful not to drift into worry, remorse, or morbid reflection, for that would diminish our usefulness to others.

8. After making our review, we seek guidance from our Higher Power as to what corrective measures need to be taken.

9. We promptly initiate such actions and make amends quickly so our joy returns and we can once again be of maximum service.

10. We continue to *watch* our internal life while releasing and surrendering the things no longer useful in our new way of living.

CHAPTER 11

Step Eleven

We sought through prayer and meditation to improve our conscious contact with God as we understood Him, praying only for the knowledge of His will for us and the power to carry that out.

News flash: God found hiding in plain sight—as everything!

We have mentioned previously the immense value of the "gift" we feel Alcoholics Anonymous has given the world with the simple idea: "God, as we understood Him."

For some who may have already had an intimate relationship with God that actually worked and bore fruit in their lives, this phrase may not have been as helpful or even needed. Yet, for those like myself, this one powerful sentence may have helped to save our lives.

Prior to reading this one line in the steps, I had never genuinely felt I had "permission" to even attempt to have a relationship with "God" *as I could understand Him,* or maybe even more importantly, as I *failed* to understand Him but deeply desired to. I could not seem to get on board with the guilt and shame-based party line of the popular hellfire-and-brimstone teachings.

Most of my life, I had been presented with what I now call "unbelievable beliefs," which I was covertly discouraged from questioning. Many apparently well-intentioned people tried to force their ideas of *God* upon me while presenting concepts that seemed foreign and even extremely contradictory to the nature of God. I somehow innately seemed to *understand* they might be slightly off the mark. Though I surely could not get my mind around the idea or magnitude of "God," common sense gifted me with knowing that if there *were* a God, His nature could not be: "He loved you one day and then threw you in a fire the next."

"Love you! But tomorrow, if you don't do what I tell you to do and believe what I tell you to believe, you'll be burning in Hell forever. Have a nice day!" (God)

Instead of *us* being made in the image and likeness of our Creator, as the story goes, it seems that we returned the favor and made a "God" in the image and likeness of *our* ego. This idea—that if someone or something doesn't do as I *dictate*, he, she, or it will incur my wrath—seemed more like something I would do to someone I was disenchanted with than something a loving Creator might do to His children.

At this moment, I want to emphatically emphasize that *I share this only to illustrate my own personal struggle with my healing and discovery of my higher power, as I am coming to understand Him, which is still ongoing. This is in no way the position of Peoples Anonymous.*

Peoples Anonymous simply encourages us to find a Power greater than ourselves that we can understand and genuinely come to believe in.

In PA, our primary objective is to stop *playing* God.

Yet, once that incredible feat is accomplished, we do begin to explore and hopefully develop a relationship with a Higher Power, whatever it may be. It is true that we were initially introduced to this idea in Step Three, but now, in Step Eleven, we are given free reign to investigate and are also motivated to spend time daily seeking conscious contact with *our* Creator.

We begin to actualize this contact by removing the blocks, first with our previous Step work and then with the daily practice of prayer and meditation. There, our inspirations are free from the judgment, distortion, or influence of anyone or anything *except* what authentically came to us in our "quiet time" with Spirit. This in no way discourages optional extracurricular activity, such as attending church, synagogues, or ashrams, or meeting with ministers, gurus, spiritual teachers, etc. What it *does* suggest, maybe even for the first time, is that we release old ideas, which may have never made sense in the first place, and embark on a distanceless journey home to the place we always were.

In Peoples Anonymous, we are allowed to seek a believable belief that works in our lives and bears the fruit of real joy.

Joy is one of the primary purposes of Peoples Anonymous and may be the only infallible indicator of the *presence* of God. For if there is a God, being in His or Her presence would surely bring joy. This is a great litmus test: if the idea or "truth" we are entertaining brings us joy, then it may be true; if it diminishes our joy, it may be false. For as God is Love, therefore He must also be joy.

We bring new ideas into our meditations upon which to ponder, for example:

God and love and joy are synonyms.

Love cannot hate.

If love *could* hate, then it may have never been *real* love in the first place.

We might also find especially helpful a prayer that we feel encompasses the truths that resonate with our souls. One that has been very helpful for some of us in the recovery movement is the Serenity Prayer:

God grant me the serenity
to accept the things I cannot change,
the courage to change the things I can,
and the wisdom to know the difference.

Amen.

What is most important in the first half of the Eleventh Step is that we take an active role in the development of our new connection with Source. We first reconciled our relationship with ourselves in Steps Four and Five; next, we began to harmonize our relationships with others in Steps Eight and Nine. In Step Ten, we continued our maintenance and house cleaning of these essential relationships and our internal spiritual condition.

In Step Eleven, we can now renovate our old ideas about God and cultivate our minds for an entirely different way of looking at the world, ourselves, those around us, and our alliance with the Higher Power.

There is a beautiful writing exercise we may also want to try in Step Eleven. It is officially named *two-way prayer*. In this spiritual exercise, after our quiet time (meditation), we take pen and paper in hand and write out our thoughts, questions, and concerns for God (in detail). Next, we invite a response to come *through us* as we listen for the reply and simply practice dictation. Some will write the questions out with one hand and the responses with the other.

We surely don't know whether what we write is actually from "God," although some of the feedback we receive in our two-way writing is quite helpful and perhaps, at minimum, comes from our "Higher Self." Research can be done on this specific exercise, and there is a vast amount of information out there if one feels compelled to pursue this practice extensively.

In Step Eleven, we do not prescribe any specific practice of meditation. We are, however, strongly encouraging each and every person in PA to find a practice that works for him or her and begin incorporating that practice into a daily spiritual program of action. The primary aim of the spiritual discipline of Step Eleven is to remind our minds that they are no longer "managers," *rulers of the world*. The mind was never created to be a governor; it was always intended as an antenna.

It is in our quiet time that we receive the guidance and inspiration necessary for the complete regeneration of our lives.

Beginning our day without this moment in the silence is similar to vigorously launching off to an unknown destination without first obtaining the address. We may eventually arrive there, although the hours wasted senselessly driving around could have been avoided had we spent a few moments downloading the address and simply plugging it into the GPS.

The second half of the Eleventh Step is an equally powerful realization. Practiced, its effect upon our lives is beyond measure.

"To pray only for the knowledge of His will for us and the Power to carry that out."

This may be one of the most spiritually advanced states of consciousness known to man.

Inherent in that simple prayer is the absolute certainty that Father knows best, and that our will and his will are one. It is the spiritual declaration that we have formally resigned from the ego's illusory tug-of-war with the Creator of all things. In its purest form, it is the acknowledgement that the desires of our hearts were placed there by our Source and therefore can and will be realized only by Him. Therefore, I pray *only* for the knowledge of His will for me and the power to carry that out, knowing that as I am about my Father's business, *he will place the desire of my heart right in my path.*

Wisdom teaches us that we don't want what we want. Nor do we perceive our own best interest in any given situation. There is no circumstance that I can but judge amiss, for my perception is at best still somewhat distorted. Fortunately, there is One who can see things clearly—and in His perception, there is no distortion.

It is in the second half of Step Eleven that we may spend the rest of our lives practicing and attaining this degree of trust, whereby we place more faith in our spiritual vision on behalf of Truth than in what our eyes report to us moment by moment.

Step Eleven Exercises

1. Begin to explore and research different types of meditation. Try to find one you can enjoy and connect with.

2. Put into daily practice your newfound meditation for at least thirty days before you decide if it's working or not.

3. Try to find some reading material that resonates with you. Take at least fifteen minutes each morning reading your new daily meditation, and remain in your quiet time for a few extra moments.

4. Give two-way writing a try, asking Source (or your higher Self) for guidance, and write out what you feel you hear or receive coming "through" you in response to your request.

5. Spend some time with the Prayer of St. Francis or the Serenity Prayer, and meditate on the powerful insights these prayers hold.

6. Discover a new activity, such as walking in the park, spending time on a beach, climbing mountains, taking a jog, etc. that for whatever reason seems to help you feel your inner connectedness to all things. Incorporate this into your regular schedule as much as possible.

7. Commit to a thirty-day period to *actually* "Pray only for knowledge of His will for you and the Power to carry that out." During this month, we cease all prayer soliciting specific outcomes in all the circumstances of our lives and the lives of others. We practice *believing* that there may be a Power that truly knows what's best in each and every situation. (We wholeheartedly relinquish the delusion that we can or ever could accomplish this). We consider this Power's Perception to be perfectly clear, encompassing all things past, present, and in the future. We ask *only* for the *knowledge* of this vision and the power to do, or not do, whatever is needed in accordance with this divine direction.

8. Fasten your seatbelt.

CHAPTER 12

Step Twelve

Having had a spiritual awakening as the result of these steps, we tried to carry this message to others and practice these principles in all of our affairs.

G ood morning. How was your nap?
Sweet dreams?

As previously stated, the Bible informs us in Genesis: "Man fell into a deep sleep and God took out a rib and made woman."

Nowhere does it ever say: "He woke up."

As a matter of fact, what comes after that "surgery" does appear, at times, to look a lot like someone having a really bad dream.

Fortunately, we will *not* attempt to understand the literal or metaphysical meaning of the remaining chapters of the Bible (or any other book for that matter). This is not the time or the place, and for the record, we of Peoples Anonymous encourage you to honor any belief that sincerely works for you, bears fruit, and brings joy to you and others. There are those who believe that even the simple placebo effect of a belief in an all-loving God has helped their lives tremendously, whether or not there actually is one.

Here, we are given full permission to not only have a God of our own understanding but also to awaken to that realization in our own space and in our own time (not that we need *permission*, but just in case, allow us to be among the first to officially offer it to you). Actually, you can work the Twelve Steps of Peoples Anonymous as an active atheist or agnostic. There have been many among us who used the group itself, in the beginning, as their higher power. Here was a group of people who, as a whole, assuredly accomplished far more than they could have individually.

The only requirement is your willingness to release old ideas that are no longer serving you and become open to new experiences in every area of your life. Most importantly, we must be willing to raise to the light of doubt some of our fundamental core beliefs. Lastly, we must be open-minded enough to merely consider that there might be a Power greater than ourselves at work in this vast universe.

We must remain open to the idea that what we *know* may not *be so.*

The failure to acknowledge this fact or even its *possibility* in any area of our lives is usually rooted in some form of arrogance, hubris, or self-righteous indignation. Let us remember that it's not what we don't know that hurts us; it's what we know that just ain't so. To operate our lives in strict accord to a belief system that may be false while vehemently refusing to consider these ideas in the light of doubt—this may be the essence of "walking in our sleep."

Step Twelve is our awakening. Here, we open our eyes, look around, and many of us exclaim, "Oh my God, what have I done?"

We of Peoples Anonymous assure you, if you have become rigorously honest with yourself about your innate personal powerlessness, if you have extracted the management of your life from the claws of the ego and placed it unreservedly in the hands of the Higher Power, if you have done an honest and thorough personal inventory and shared it with God and another human being, if you have asked your Creator to remove the shortcomings blocking you from the sunlight of the Spirit and your usefulness to others, and if you have begun making amends for your past, the great news of this program is that the best years of your life lie ahead, no matter your present circumstances, and by practicing these spiritual principles in *all* of your affairs, you shall realize a life beyond your wildest dreams.

Our awakening is usually evident to those around us long before it is evident to us. We begin to see a reflection of this work in our lives as we practice the spiritual principles of these steps in all of our affairs.

What *are* the twelve principles of the Twelve Steps?

1. Honesty
2. Hope
3. Faith
4. Courage
5. Integrity
6. Willingness
7. Humility
8. Discipline
9. Forgiveness/Brotherly Love
10. Acceptance
11. Perseverance/Awareness
12. Service/Gratitude

In our sleep, we may have valued the valueless. As we awaken in Step Twelve, we begin to discover the things in life that truly are of great value.

I was once directed: "If you want to know what is of value, close your eyes."

What do you see with your eyes closed?

Do you notice anything that will last forever?

What lasts forever?

Next, I was asked, "If we are eternal beings, what true value is there in gaining something we will ultimately lose? What can be taken with us wherever we go?"

I remember when I first began this process of recovery and was searching for things of value in my life. I acutely remember that when I closed my eyes, I saw nothing. As the journey has continued, I have begun to notice some of the greatest gifts: things that, honestly, I would have previously overlooked. These are, to me, the greatest treasures of life and the things I can now see with my eyes closed and take with me wherever I go.

This short list may contain some of the aspirations of an "awakened life," and the gifts of Peoples Anonymous:

1. Peace of mind
2. Real joy inside my own skin
3. Integrity with my *true self* and others
4. A sense of purpose
5. A sense of accomplishment
6. A sense of belonging
7. Moments of bliss
8. Real Love
9. Beauty
10. Certainty
11. Connectedness
12. Restitution

As you continue to do this work, please feel free to compile your own list of the things you discover along the way that are of great value, many of which you *may* have overlooked in your previous life.

Therefore, having had a spiritual awakening as a result of these steps, having begun to practice these spiritual principles in all of our affairs, and having had some genuine discoveries of what is truly meaningful in life, we are now in a position to attempt to transmit what we have been given so freely.

In conclusion, let us address:

"We tried to carry this message to others."

This, my friends, is the moment of truth, when we truly launch off on a lifelong course of action while sincerely dedicating our lives to the service of our Employer by becoming willing to completely shift our paradigm, from the world's teaching:

"Take care of ourselves first, and then, if there are any resources left over, share what remains with our brothers and sisters."

to:

"Spend the first fruits of our time and energy attempting to transform the lives of those around us who have been entrusted to our care."

Many will be literally placed in our path, or we shall encounter them by actively seeking the lost, the broken, the hurting, the sick, the bewildered, the confused, the disappointed, the ripe, and, hopefully, the *ready*.

In Peoples Anonymous, when we have had a transformation, a genuine healing in any area of our lives—mind, body or spirit, physically, mentally, or emotionally; be it from depression, cancer, some other form of sickness, trauma, heartbreak, divorce, financial problems, or from simply living our lives with a lack of joy—we launch off on a strategic course of action to find others with similar difficulties so that our lives can bear witness, through attraction rather than promotion, to the Power accessible through these Twelve Steps.

We know that if we take care of the children of the universe, the universe will in turn take care of us.

I had previously spent my life in strict accord with the fundamental premise passed down to me through the ages: take care of yourself and your family; then, in your spare time, always be willing to help others. I operated my life in adherence to this belief system, genuinely thinking I was doing the right thing.

I happened to notice, while I was attempting to take care of myself that the Universe was busy taking care of you.

I saw some of you apparently being better taken care of than me, although simply noticing this phenomenon was not sufficient to cause the necessary shift.

It was only when I dedicated my life to the service of others—I might mention, *only because my life literally depended on it*—that I stumbled upon this profound principle:

If I sincerely spend my time, my talents, my money, and my energy assisting others in the transformation of their lives, the Universe will ensure I have *all I need* to not only fulfill my mission but bring to me the desires of my heart to demonstrate the power of this program so that my Employer's kids might know there is a way out *that actually works.*

We will know them by their fruits.

The fruit of this work, from the simple joy of living a life on purpose, to the bliss we experience by having a front-row seat to the transformation of a human life while *knowing* we were a small catalyst of that healing, all the way to the spiritual, mental, physical, and financial realization of our dreams, turns our lives into a living example of *carrying this message to others.*

When we are approached by those who may be in need of our help, simply because they have heard the "music of our lives," or we have found those who were hurting, we *go to work.*

The great secret in working with others is to not let them drain our time and energy "talking about the screen."

That is where they usually initially believe the problem exists. There is a short moment in the beginning when it is necessary and even helpful to allow them to do this just long enough for you to gain an understanding of the gravity of the problem and what brought them to a place of willingness and hopefully to enough desperation to heal their lives.

The moment these key ingredients are apparent and as soon as the person has expressed willingness to *go to any lengths for healing*, we immediately focus all of our attention on the cause of the problem: *the projector* (the mind that is casting their experience onto the screens they call their lives).

Just for the record, this is the place where all problems exist, and coincidentally, the only place that even recognizes the word *problem*. We must refuse to allow anyone to draw us off course by appealing to the part of our nature that likes to play junior counselor, therapist, financial advisor, marriage counselor, teacher, healer, guru, etc.

When the technology states that *no human power* can relieve the ultimate cause of our problems—the selfishness and self-centeredness that is at the core of our dis-ease and disharmony with life—I'm afraid, that includes *me*.

As hard as it may be for some of us to grasp, "no human power" means *no human power*. Last I checked, we all fall under that category. This may sound silly and even an overstatement of the obvious, but for those of us who spend our lives in the trenches attempting to help others, this is *very* important to remember. Hopefully, we will be reminded of this when we stray off the beam with excessive vigilance.

With this recipe, the real work lies in *the action* the individual takes though working these steps. This helps them feel like they took part in the solution, for which they can honestly take responsibility. They can even have a small amount of healthy pride in actively participating in the transformation of their lives. We simply walk them *through the steps*.

Word by word, page by page, step by step. No bright ideas, nothing added, nothing altered, nothing deleted—for *nothing* else is needed.

Why not?

Because the Recipe actually works. It *really* does.

This spiritual technology, followed precisely, has transformed the lives of millions of alcoholics, addicts, overeaters, gamblers, sex addicts, potheads, codependents, and many other spiritually, financially, and emotionally bankrupted people.

We are certain that the Power that those of us in recovery throughout the world have gained by utilizing the Twelve Steps is eagerly available for the rest of the people on the planet.

Once Again,
We Welcome You To Peoples Anonymous

May the day come when if anyone, anywhere reaches out
for the hand of PA, someone with personal experience of
transformation will be there. May the gatherings spring up
throughout the world for those who are earnestly seeking healing
to always have a group to call home. May the rest of the world
be as richly blessed as those of us who are currently active in
other Twelve-Step programs, knowing we are never alone.

Step Twelve Exercises

1. May we begin to practice these principles in all our affairs.

2. When we fall short (which we will surely do), simply apply the Tenth Step by "continuing to take our inventory and, when we're wrong, promptly admit it, make amends quickly if harm is caused, and immediately turn our thoughts to someone we can help."

3. Know that we don't know. No matter which side of the pendulum we happen to swing, whether we feel qualified or even expert in our field of helping others, or whether, at times, we feel totally inadequate, *realize we cannot fix ourselves or others.* Every time we sit with a new man or woman to begin this work, may we pray:

   Dad, I got nothing, so if you don't show up, we are both in worlds of trouble.

   or:

   I am here only to be truly helpful.
   I am here to represent Him Who sent me.
   I do not have to worry about what to say or what to do, because He Who sent me will direct me.
   I am content to be wherever He wishes, knowing He goes there with me.
   I will be healed as I let Him teach me to heal.
   (T-2.V.A.18:2-6)

4. Only a Power greater than ourselves can transform the human life. We must always remember this. Our job is to help plug them into the Source and then get out of their way.

5. We must always remain teachable as we continue to do this work. We continue to grow in understanding and effectiveness. We allow ourselves time to master the transmission of this technology, while always knowing no act of kindness—no matter how large or small, no energy spent in the service of our brothers and sisters—is ever wasted.

Epilogue

This book is a beginning, not an end. Always keep an open mind to experience strength and hope from those who have been working these steps successfully with regard to the various ways you can continue to apply them to your life. The exercises enclosed merely scratch the surface of a lifelong journey. I honestly do not believe that this book will ultimately become the basic text for Peoples Anonymous, but it is my hope that this chip of a book will be a spark that the world will fan into a flame that becomes a movement where, finally, all are welcome.

Some day, the first hundred members of PA, like the first hundred members of AA, may get together and construct their own volume. Until then, *you are welcome to use mine.*

PA is not a marriage between a Course in Miracles and the Twelve Steps, but it is assuredly an intimate relationship. May this union of these two incredibly beautiful spiritual technologies help bring healing and recovery into the twenty-first century.

There are no words to express my gratitude to the One who entrusted me with this task. Honestly, I felt there were many far more qualified. It is my only hope that my Employer (Dad) is well pleased. If I lived a million years, I could not begin to repay the gifts that have been so freely given me as the direct result of being able to finally access my Higher Power through these Twelve Steps.

I am happy to report that after working the Steps for many years, *they now work me.* When a problem arises, as they surely do from time to time, my natural instinct *now* is to immediately admit my powerlessness and surrender the situation unreservedly. Next, I come to believe that a Power greater than myself, as long as I don't get involved, will restore my life to sanity, balance, beauty, and joy. Then, I turn the situation wholeheartedly over to the care of God, *as I still don't fully understand Him.* Next, I make a searching and fearless inventory of myself, searching for my part in the co-creation of the problem at hand. I am always the prime suspect. Fortunately, it does not usually take me long to discover when I have made a decision based on self that has placed me at the scene of the crime or in a position to be hurt. Then, with the same desperation that I cried out with all those years ago, I petition my Source to remove from me the defects of character that were *ultimately* at cause. When I sincerely want relief, I make amends quickly and turn my thoughts to someone I can help. Next, I seek through prayer and meditation to improve my conscious contact with God, praying only for the knowledge of His will for me and the power to carry that out.

This is simply how we apply this beautiful way of life to our life on a daily basis once we have worked our steps.

In the Twelve-Step program that I *grew up in public* in, we used to say, "All it takes to start a meeting is two people, a coffee pot, and a resentment." We are told from another fellowship, "When two or more come together in my name, I am there." We of Peoples Anonymous encourage the gathering of like-minded souls with a common purpose. There is no place in the universe more powerful than where any two or more come together, fully recognizing their interests are not separate. If one wins, the other wins; if one loses, they all lose.

Following are the Twelve Traditions, which by the sheer grace of God have made it possible for some of the most selfish and self-centered people on the planet to coexist in harmony for over eighty years. I am confident that they will also work beautifully for Peoples Anonymous.

FYI: *The Twelve Steps and Twelve Traditions* book published by Alcoholics Anonymous World Service, Inc. is considered a great asset also available to those interested in further study who can set aside the *alcoholic* terminology and gain from the tremendous insights therein.

The Twelve Traditions of Peoples Anonymous

1. Our common welfare should come first; personal recovery depends upon PA unity.
2. For our group purpose there is but one ultimate authority—a loving God as He may express Himself in our group conscience. Our leaders are but trusted servants; they do not govern.
3. The only requirement for PA membership is a desire to transform your life.
4. Each group should be autonomous except in matters affecting other groups or PA as a whole.
5. Each group has but one primary purpose—to carry its message to others who still suffer.
6. A PA group ought never endorse, finance, or lend the PA name to any related facility or outside enterprise, lest problems of money, property, and prestige divert us from our primary purpose.
7. Every PA group ought to be fully self-supporting, declining outside contributions.
8. Peoples Anonymous should remain forever nonprofessional, but our service centers may employ special workers.
9. PA, as such, ought never be organized; but we may create service boards or committees directly responsible to those they serve.
10. Peoples Anonymous has no opinion on outside issues; hence the PA name ought never be drawn into public controversy.
11. Our public relations policy is based on attraction rather than promotion; we need always maintain personal anonymity at the level of press, radio, and films.
12. Anonymity is the spiritual foundation of all our traditions, ever reminding us to place principles before personalities.

Let us always remember on our very best day this is still simply spiritual kindergarten. We never graduate. No matter where we are or how long we've been in the program, we never become more spiritually advanced than when we *chop wood and carry water.*

SELECTED AWAKENINGS
AND THE AUTHOR'S
CLOSING THOUGHTS

Here we have a sprinkling of various stories of
healing and transformation written anonymously by
several different members of Twelve-Step groups
across the country, including a few of the original
members of Peoples Anonymous and the author's note.

Peace, Love, and Understanding

I t was 1962. Mom was twenty-two years old and I was her fifth and last child. Mom and dad divorced in my first year of life. My father never bothered paying child support, but mom was determined to be the best at raising us kids. She went to school while working two jobs, which caused her to be away from us most of the time. This was rough on me, because the only time I felt safe was in her arms. I loved her smell and her warm skin and the way she loved on me. I lived each day waiting for her to come through that door. During this time, my grandparents helped raise us, and I was left with them quite often. The environment was fanatically religious and often abusive, to say the least. The evangelist Billy Graham was always on the TV with the volume blaring twenty-four hours a day. There was nowhere I could go in the large six-bedroom, two-story house to find silence or peace. My grandmother ruled with an iron fist and wore way too much perfume. The smell was suffocating. I was petrified of her: when I heard her coming, I would hide in one of the many closets out of fear of punishment—for what, I did not know, but I knew it was coming. Beatings, hot sauce in my mouth, restraints, and being locked away in an upstairs room when mom left the house was a daily routine. I honestly don't remember my older siblings being around much. While my siblings were out of the house, I often hid in my mom's closet with her scent, out of reach of granny.

We were raised strict fire-and-brimstone southern Baptist till I was seven, and I have the physical and emotional scars to prove it. Then, mom got married to husband number three. Suddenly, I found myself in a Jewish family, and I was cast as an actress in the play, *The Fiddler on The Roof.* A short time after this, I became a Jewish Center summer counselor. Within months of their marriage, we were the front-page news. Mom became the president of the Women's Jewish Community Center. I remember spinning inside my own mind just trying to keep up. I had to fit in quickly, or I would disappear into my own sense of abandonment and fearful mind. The world around me, at times, was really freaking me out.

My siblings, during this time, were having fun putting illegal drugs into my little body while sexually abusing me. I was learning, very early on, to "roll with things" for my sheer survival. I often felt surrounded by strangers, in a constant state of fear and isolation. I remember longing for the protection and nurturing of my mommy! Was this the way life was supposed to be? I didn't know. "Mommy" was the only thing that made sense to me. But she was continuously gone, trying to survive and raise five kids. I couldn't breathe without her. I felt like I was a piece of raw meat in a pack of wolves without her scent around to protect me. I watched her often get beaten by the men in her life, and I couldn't save her. "I am worthless!" was my silent, isolated scream.

My relationship with God started very young. I loved God. As sunrays danced around me through the branches of the trees, I knew God was playing with me in my little private gardens. Until the beatings, abandonment and sexual abuse, I truly thought God loved me, too. Then, as the days, weeks and years passed, I hid my face in utter shame and embarrassment when I began to believe that God saw me as dirty, and the idea that I was a mistake sank deep into the very fiber of my being. The pain of simply existing was overwhelming, and I was stuck in this strange world to which I felt I did not belong. Somewhere inside my mind, I slammed shut the door to this outside world that I did not know how to survive in. I was powerless, full of shame, and I was hurt. Most of the time, all I could do was manage to get through each day attempting to somehow tolerate the pain I felt inside. I quickly learned to form a larger-than-life personality: I would walk into a room with a smile, so people would not see my shame, pretending to like people but never knowing how to feel close to them. They all laughed together and seemed to have fun. So, I pretended to laugh and have fun too. Soon, my life was beginning to look like I was "fitting in" just fine, but I never felt I actually did. I was an overachiever stuck in the fantasy that someday, someone would recognize a purpose for me. I would act as if I didn't care what anyone thought of me. I couldn't sit still in one place for too long, and I was always trying to find anything that would distract me from the pain of being *myself*. I became adept at being whoever I needed to be to survive any given moment. Role models? I had the dark ones. Drugs, sex and rock and roll. If I wasn't feeling, it was a good day.

I escaped most of the physical and emotional pain by becoming top of my class in academics and sports. I found ways to control the external world around me, as early as elementary school. By third grade, I was captain of the dodge ball team. For some reason, the boys always wanted to corner me on the playground and beat me up. They may have been threatened by my air of false confidence. By then, I had already lost all ability to feel tribal or a part of something. When I was motivated in some direction, I would focus only on the goal at hand and put blinders on against the outside world. I couldn't relate to others' feelings and certainly didn't think anyone cared about mine. I was constantly comparing my insides to other people's outsides. In middle and high school, the sexual abuse continued, but I was growing stronger. I stayed away from home and out of my neighborhood as much as possible. No one ever really looked for me, but I was usually on a basketball or tennis court, practicing till midnight. Often, I was hanging out with the misfits, doing stupid stuff like smoking cigarettes till we puked, swimming till we were waterlogged, or throwing water balloons at passing cars. I experimented as a teenager with LSD and found it to be the absolute most freeing, uninhibited feeling in the world. For the first time in my life, I could breathe, and I felt whole, as if I belonged in this cosmic universe. But I saw a friend have a terrible trip, and my hope turned back into hopelessness.

Around my seventeenth year, during my mom's fourth marriage, my lack of self worth and the hopelessness I felt drove me to slice the veins of my wrists while sitting alone in my apartment. Fortunately, the blade did not puncture deep enough, as the bleeding of my skin started to freak me out. In that instant, I really didn't know if I wanted to die or just needed some major nurturing. I was crying for someone to please *see me*. On another occasion, I punched my fist through a glass door. It sliced my hand up pretty bad, but it felt amazing, because it caused me not to feel my internal unmanageable emotional pain, which was my constant companion, just for a moment. I suffered through most of these self-infliction episodes alone.

Later that year, I discovered scuba diving. Oh, my soul. For the second time in my life, I could breathe. We traveled the islands, ate freshly caught fish, and explored underwater paradises. The only problem: I had to eventually surface. When I wasn't diving, I was swimming. I loved the feeling of being in water. It made me feel alive.

Then, mom got a divorce. The landscape of my life was again deteriorating right before my eyes, and I had absolutely no hope to stand on. I spun out of control, either overworking, overachieving, medicating myself to sleep (and sometimes into the waking hours), or just simply sitting in a dark closet, wondering if anyone was looking for me. Call it what you will—depression, bipolar, or just bat-shit crazy—the label really doesn't matter. I was void of any sense of purpose on this planet and saw no reason to stay. I just wanted to go back to my Maker and reevaluate what the original game plan was supposed to be for my life, because this sure the hell wasn't it.

As I was turning eighteen, I met a "spiritual guru." For the next thirty years of my life, things got really intense. The spiritual group was one hundred to two hundred people at any given time. I was the teacher's personal assistant and body worker. He required my constant time and attention and pretty much controlled all aspects of my life. In my spare time, I tried to run my own healing center. Although his techniques were harsh and confrontational, I was getting attention. I was feeling valued; I was a part of something bigger than my unmanageable feeling of shame and worthlessness. I got the best training in healing modalities and meditation. And for the first time, I felt like I was good at something. I was in my own skin and I was alive. It wasn't easy being around the guru, because his need to control bordered on emotional abuse. As intense as it all was, I was grateful I was *getting attention*, and my life had some direction. The teacher always isolated me from the group. My purpose in life was to be the best personal assistant and yogi I could be. I loved the meditation; it was better than LSD, and I fell in love with God again.

However, the guru markedly changed for the worse. He began shaming me in public and discounting my feelings. And, his twenty-four-hour-a-day unreasonable expectations wore me down emotionally and physically. Once again, I lost my feeling of connectedness and purpose. I left.

In the next few years, I wandered around aimlessly, because I didn't know how, once again, to direct my own life. I had no idea who I was nor what my purpose might be. I was always in a perpetual search for myself and what I was supposed to be doing.

Over the next decade, I went into hospitals and institutions, seeking help for my depression, mental isolation, and cult programming. Because of my thirty years of spiritual brainwashing, it was immensely hard for me to listen to any therapeutic suggestions, because I had been taught by the "guru" that any idea other than his method of "knowing God within me" fell short of the ultimate truth of God. I found myself extremely sad that I had lost my ability to meditate, as meditation had been my source of joy. This was because every time I thought of God, I would equate God with the teachings of the guru. I was unable to embrace outside help, as the guru had taught me that I was a spiritually elite, consciously awakened person. No license on the wall could teach me more than that, right?

Boy, was I screwed.

Nothing was bringing me relief. My world hit rock bottom. My relationships were falling apart. I couldn't stay focused at work and was put on a four-week personal leave and sent to see another psychiatrist. I was drinking and doing anything that would get me away from my feelings. I was isolating myself from the world, I was in emotional turmoil constantly, I was inspired to do nothing, I was worthless once again, and I was wallowing in a cesspool of self pity.

I was pulled over by the police for some reckless behavior, and in that instant, I knew that I was spiraling out of control fast, and I was terrified. I was convinced now that if I didn't get some kind of help I was going to be in serious trouble.

I called an old friend because I knew he and his family were doing well. They were such a wonderful demonstration of balance and love and always had lots of friends celebrating the joy of life around them. He had the kind of life I wanted. We scheduled to meet to have a long talk and catch up. He had always been a stand-up guy with me and had a beautiful, sincere heart. I opened up to him about myself and my troubles. He listened and genuinely heard my cry of desperation for a deeper understanding of what this thing called life was really all about.

My friend opened up to me about his past and the hardships he had overcome. He told me that he had also hit bottom in the past and had thought his life was over as well. This comforted me a great deal. He shared some personal stories with me about his own soul-searching, visits to institutions, and looking for his purpose in life. I could relate. He also was willing to share how some of his decisions in life had also taken him to some very dark places.

He then informed me that he had found a formula for living that had absolutely changed his life beyond his "wildest wet dreams." I became quite interested in what he had found and was curious about whether *that* was what had put the light in his eyes.

He spoke to me of a precise formula. The recipe was the Twelve-Step program. Having already experienced the emotional lows that came from my spiritual deprivation, I looked at my friend as he was talking about these Twelve Steps and God and literally screamed:

"You have got to be kidding me with this God stuff! There is *no* God that gives a crap about me. I have *been around* Twelve-Step programs for over thirty years, and either they are flawed, or I am, because it certainly hasn't helped me!"

He calmly asked me if ever, *in the last thirty years*, I had followed all of the Twelve-Step formula, word by word, page by page, doing exactly what it said, precisely as it was written. I was quick to say no. Never precisely.

He told me that if I would follow this recipe exactly, *as it is written*, doing all the things it said to *do* and not doing any of the things it said *not* to do, that he guaranteed my life would be more beautiful than I could ever imagine. He *guaranteed* my success if I would follow the recipe in the exact fashion he had! This got my attention. The experience he was having working the Twelve Steps in his own life was enough to give me great hope, all I needed was to give it a try.

Together, we launched out on a course of action. We met half a dozen times over the next three weeks, studying every line of the book. Because of his work with these Steps, my friend had an amazing clarity and brought great insight as to what they meant. For the first time in my life, I started to understand how unmanageable my mind and emotions truly were. I saw how far beyond human aid I had become. My friend and I walked into the light of the Third Step, seeing along the ways the tricks my mind had been playing on me and how God had been there all along, waiting for me to *humbly* show up. I was challenged to set aside all of the religious beliefs of my upbringing for a moment, including the Guru's beliefs, and come to *my own understanding about God*. This rocked my world. In my Third Step, I turned over all of my confusion about myself and about life to a loving and powerfully present God. My heart completely opened inside, and I felt a power flow in. For the first time in my life, I took a breath from God. I understood that *that* breath was God given, just for me, His beloved child. Finally, in a wholly instant, I had a personal relationship that felt so intimate, inside me, for me. I was elated and filled with such a tremendous, indescribable joy. All the self-inflicted spiritual maladies of worthlessness, purposelessness, separateness, isolation, sadness and so on, were gone.

Now, with God guiding me in the Third Step, I surrendered my life and will over to His care as I launched into the Fourth Step. I undertook a very honest and intense look at all of my resentments with life, people and God that I had carried for so many years. Boy, was I surprised at what I found. I scraped the bottom. It was painful but freeing. Also, by sharing and examining these resentments with another person, my friend whom I trusted, I began to understand how sometimes I had created these situations myself, and the pain had resulted from my own actions. Wow. That was a wake-up call. Not only had I been hurt, but I had actually inflicted pain on others through my selfishness and self-centeredness. Somehow, I felt free in knowing this about myself. I certainly had endured a lot of hardship, but now, I was feeling *me*: what I had become inside my own skin. Maybe it wasn't pretty in some areas, but it was honest.

Steps Six and Seven were another major turning point for me. After Step Five, telling my whole life story in the presence of God and another human being, I found a secluded place to sit for one hour with God. It was explained to me that one hour meant one hour. Remembering the formula will only work if I follow it precisely, I was reminded, and fifty-nine minutes was not one hour. So I turned off my phone and set my alarm for sixty minutes. The instructions told me to review the last Five Steps. I started to read each step I had done thus far, I knew my life and thoughts had become unmanageable and that everyone who had tried to help me before couldn't seem to get through. I truly felt that I now had an amazing personal connection to a God of my understanding; this had taken only five minutes. What was I to do with the next fifty-five minutes?

I turned my mind back to God, as a child learns to take her first steps across the floor into daddy's arms. Then, it happened. The voice "inside of my heart" spoke louder than my own restless mind. It told me to open my notebook and start writing. I did. What happened on those pages over the next fifty minutes is far beyond words. God showed up, and my heart felt again as if it were resuscitated. I had no more shame and nothing to hide. God was seeing me as I was: good.

Yes, I had done some harm to others. In Step Eight, I got honest again. With God's help, I wrote that list, without omitting a single person that I had harmed. My friend helped me look at the harms that I had felt I had caused to see if indeed they were real and I truly did need to make an amends. In Step Nine, I set out to clean up the wreckage of my past and to make amends to those I had harmed. I did this fearlessly with the courage of God that was directing me. I came to see that all beings are children of God. I accepted my responsibility and became accountable to those I had harmed by making direct amends to them. It was a phenomenal process.

My life now is literally amazing. The guarantee my friend made to me continues to be true, beyond my wildest dreams. I live each day in the principles of Steps Ten through Twelve. I wake to see God's sun rise each morning on the horizon of the ocean, through the window of my house. I hear God's voice in the ebb and flow of the waves caressing the shore. I sit in deep gratitude and yes, even in meditation, each morning, loving this gift of life I have been given. When I am wrong, I try to be quick to admit it and continue to ask God to keep revealing His purpose for me in His world. I am born anew each day as I pray and meditate and attempt to align my mind to His will.

I have been blessed with an amazing partner and see God's love for me every time I look into her eyes. I didn't know that one day my heart would feel so much love for another person. We have a beautiful home and very successful ocean-based business together. I am blessed to be back in the water sharing my love of the ocean with others each day. Our days are spent helping people on so many levels: In my spare time, I have also earned my master's degree and am now a reverend working with others through prayer, meditation, Twelve-Step sponsorship, and spiritual counseling. I am so grateful to be a demonstration of God's love each day. I feel so blessed to finally understand my purpose now.

Sometimes, that extra-special person comes around who has been beaten down by life, and I smile. I smile because I know God has put them here for me to love. I smile because I now possess the formula given so freely to me by my friend. I smile because I know there is a way out. I smile because I, too, can guarantee that extra-special person that if he or she follows these Twelve-Step directions precisely, they also can have a life beyond their wildest wet dreams!

I am very grateful that this beautiful recipe not only saved my life but also gave me a life beyond anything I could have ever imagined, is now available to the rest of the world through Peoples Anonymous.

Healing Touch

My childhood was happy while I was growing up in a middle-class 1970s California way. Not perfect, not awful, not terribly unique. There was a pervasive shallowness that was cultural and all encompassing; I struggled against it because I really knew nothing else. At the time, I could not name it: I just knew something was amiss. Adolescence was hard for me, as it is for most. All the usual bumps in the road, rebellions, and embarrassments. I can remember the moment when that vague discontentment with the way things were migrated into depression. I was at the age when you begin to question the world, conceive of and contemplate death for the first time—that age when you first look around, recognize yourself as one of many and begin to question your purpose and role within this vast universe.

I was around sixteen years old when it all really hit me. Up until that point, I was a champion athlete. However, I had stopped enjoying it and was only going through the motions because it was what everyone else wanted me to be. Then, I finally just let go. I gave up; I quit. I stopped swimming and started smoking weed and was experimenting with other drugs and alcohol. In my attempt to define myself in a world filled with people too busy *defining* themselves to listen much, I began to feel increasingly adrift and ambiently discontented.

I discovered that I had a powerful singing voice and was a really good mimic. This caused the local bar bands to begin asking me to sit in. Unfortunately, I now had the rock-and-roll lifestyle right there offering me a new kind of escape. Increasingly, my *world* began to disapprove of my life choices. I went from golden child to misfit. I began to realize the world was a much crueler, uglier place than the TV had led me to believe. I began asking questions no one could or would answer. I could not articulate my feelings and ideas without fear of judgment or disapproval from my peers and family. During this time of my life, my first boyfriend, who also happened to be my first sexual partner, betrayed me, *and that sealed the deal.* I completely lost faith in the world and in myself.

My depression was further complicated because, at the beginning at least, it wasn't chemical. Initially, it was circumstantial, situational, and unrecognized by anyone around me. I felt devastated at what I thought the world was, what it appeared people *only* cared about, and how selfish and self-absorbed everyone was. I began to hang around with those I considered "my kind": the cynics and misfits, who, I'm afraid, only made these feelings more compounded and severe. I was very empathic and extremely sensitive, which was seen as a sign of weakness. I have come to learn that these qualities actually require a tremendous amount of strength.

I covered all this up by frequently being a clown, acting like a fool, and making people laugh with or, usually, at me. I had many highs and lows, and was at times ridiculously out of control in my attempt to deny what I saw as the fatality and futility of it all. I found myself playing on the sympathy of others whenever I could and becoming more and more manipulative than I ever wanted to admit to myself. This led to all the usual unhealthy coping mechanisms: bad relationships, sex, food, drugs, alcohol ... I vainly attempted suicide around nineteen, really just to cry for help.

I was drowning in hedonism, and after I got out of the hospital, I felt even worse about myself when I realized how many people I had hurt with my selfishness, directly and indirectly.

I had two kids by the age of twenty-two, and I genuinely did the best I could for them, while I was struggling just to keep my head above water. I entered into a hasty second marriage in my late twenties, in which the two of us acted out all of our insecurities almost on a daily basis. It became extremely emotionally abusive on both sides. This relationship finally pushed me into therapy, where I found some relief, briefly. I did the work that was suggested as best I could, but the environment I had created for myself was not conducive to getting well, so I was never really able to make lasting changes. My spiritual malady manifested further as I completely lost faith in people, I was continuously confused by the world, and I eventually became incapable of managing my life. It was safer to outsource to my family, or husband—I was always putting the solution outside of me. Men, food, alcohol, sex, moving to a new place, finding a new job, etc. Always external.

My second husband bullied me into having one last child, and thank God he did. This was the beginning of the end. When the last little one showed up, I realized I had to get him, and my older two children out, fast. I was suffering from severe postpartum depression, but every time I tried to reach out to my husband in an attempt to communicate that I needed *some kind of help*, all he would do was threaten me. Something had to give. I drank a lot then—to keep up with him, to save my marriage, because when I was sober, I fully realized the nightmare I had trapped my children and myself in. I saw absolutely no way out. Every ounce of energy and faith was being drained away as I continued to stay. I was once again becoming suicidal, and there was nowhere to turn. Finally, my children's godmother gave me an ultimatum: Get out of this marriage, or she would call CPS.

I was not angry; nor did I become defensive. I was utterly broken by then. I intuitively knew that I couldn't do it on my own; she told me what to do, and I did it.

Those post-marriage days are dark and hard to revisit. Heartbroken doesn't even begin to express my feelings; annihilated with absolutely no identity left might be closer. After one more very brief and very ugly rebound relationship, I fell on my knees and prayed to God for help.

I somehow managed to put myself through night school as a massage therapist and found I had an unusual skill. Healing and working on others did take a bit of the edge off of my own shattered sense of self. It dulled the sharp edges of my depression, but didn't cure it. I was just "sick and tired of being sick and tired" as they say; I was tired of being a victim, tired of the shame, the humiliation, the discontent, and the self-loathing. That's when I met some friends who first told me about Peoples Anonymous— the Twelve Steps available for anyone who really wants to be well.

I began the process only because I had absolutely nowhere else to turn. None of the usual bad coping mechanisms were working anymore. The steps terrified me: to accept full responsibility for everything that brought me to this point? To let go of my resentments and forgive?

I remember a panicked moment of sheer terror at who I would be if I didn't have *my story*, no longer having the people who I blamed to hold me up and justify my mediocre existence. But, as I mentioned before, I was so desperate, I was willing to try anything. I was completely out of *bright ideas*—and the Twelve Steps entirely changed my life.

Through this process, I found that being fully present and conscious is wonderful when you can see the world as it is, with all of its exquisite truths and tremendous beauty. As I ripped off the Band-Aid of drama and victimhood, my own conscience became clear, and I began to make better choices for myself. I quit drinking and smoking marijuana, became vegan, started doing yoga and meditating, and found a wonderful support system that has allowed me to maintain a depression-free life.

You see, the steps helped me to discover that the meaning of life that had eluded me for so many years was right in front of me the entire time: we are here for each other. We are here to love and live together, to see the beauty and

**majesty in each other, and to lift each other up, knowing
that someone will always be there to lift us up as well.**

The interconnectedness of everything—life, love, God—it's all there, and it's all one. I was just too busy being upset that the world and its people were not what I wanted them to be, what I felt they should be, *to see it*.

If you follow the Twelve Steps exactly, you cannot fail, because the process will completely unravel absolutely everything you thought you knew about yourself. It will help you uncover your true beauty and purpose that lies underneath all of the *ugliness* you have used to get by.

**I know it is *me* that has since changed, but I swear the
world that I see now *is* the one I always wanted it to be.**

I changed my perspective through working the Twelve Steps, and in so doing, I have found tranquility, abundance, peace, and a completely transformed life. Thank God for the Twelve Steps, and for the fact that they are finally available to everyone through Peoples Anonymous.

From Abandoned to Healer

My story begins with being raised by two separate mothers who were both drinking alcoholics. My birth mother raised me until I was a little over two years old and then abandoned me. I lived for a short time in foster care and then was taken in by a family who had two sons, six and seven years older than me. My adoptive mother desperately wanted a little girl but did not want to go through another pregnancy. At first, she was thrilled with who I was and the talents I brought with me. But then, as time went by, I began to experience mental, physical, and sexual abuse. I began to have my own ideas about things, and a great deal of animosity grew between us. She often told me that my birth mother didn't want me, that she was white trash, and unless I worked really hard I would be nothing but white trash, too. In her eyes, I seesawed between being the extraordinary child she wanted and being an absolute failure at everything I tried. A week after I turned seventeen, I eloped with my boyfriend. I was three months pregnant at the time. That marriage produced my first son and was over within six months.

Back home with my adoptive parents, I lived the life of a single mother. I had dropped out of high school and become a very resourceful and skillful liar. I was able to obtain employment right away as a secretary and manager of a small business, because I lied about having graduated from high school. At my next job interview, I added that I had one year of college. The next job, I learned to be a paralegal, which afforded me the ability to get several other pretty good jobs. As time went by, I kept adding more years of college to my *so-called* educational background.

At nineteen, I began to "party." I had an extreme sense of entitlement, since I had "been through so much in my life." I felt I had the absolute right to enjoy myself. I took my son to daycare and went to work every day, so I felt I deserved to party. It quickly got out of hand.

I began to sleep around, get terribly into debt, and generally just destroy my and my son's lives. I moved to do what we call a *geographical* (when you try to run from yourself and your problems by moving to a different location, thinking things will be *better)* from the small town where I resided to a much larger city where I managed to keep it together fairly well for the first year. Then, I began to party again. I lost my job and began to procrastinate looking for another one, writing multiple checks on an empty bank account in the meantime. I ended up getting caught and spent a month in jail, waiting to go to court. In court, I was given eighteen months of probation with the stipulation that I get another job, pay off the checks and keep my "nose clean." This lasted about six weeks, and I ended up back in my hometown hospital with a suicide attempt under my belt.

My dear, sweet adoptive father first brought me the message of Twelve-Step recovery at that time, but I was horrified to think that he thought I was in need of such help. Due to my biases, I wasn't interested in what he had to offer at that time. After getting out of the hospital, I hooked up with my next husband and we were married within eight weeks (this lasted for the next nine years). He adopted my son, and together, we had two daughters. My dis-ease with life (as well as his) became more pronounced and more damaging to everybody around us in those nine years. It was at the end of that period, after my second divorce, that I was introduced to the Twelve-Step family program. At the time, I had ceased drinking, but I was heavily medicated by three different doctors. As time passed, I became less and less capable of being *anything* like a good mother, competent employee, or citizen of the world. I was then encouraged to go into the original Twelve-Step program I was introduced to in May of 1972 by my adoptive father. That's when I finally began to live within, and apply to my life, the principles of the Twelve Steps.

Of course, I was already with another man, and for the record, very co-dependently involved. Yet, I will forever be grateful for his part in my story. He was, like me, bright, resourceful, and intelligent. He knew the literature of recovery, cover to cover, and could teach it like no other. But he himself could not live in the principles of the program. The relationship ended after two years. By then, I could clearly see that I was powerless over my beliefs from my past. I knew both instinctively and spiritually that any substance, person, or circumstance I used to change my feelings would cloud my ability to recognize and act on truth. In those two years, I abstained from alcohol and drugs but indulged in sex, love, and rock and roll. Again, my life became a chaotic mess, especially around handling my finances.

Eventually, I began to learn to live life on life's terms. It was during this time that I truly committed to trying to understand all I could about a power greater than myself and to use that power to sincerely begin the healing process. I was gifted with wonderful, wise teachers from the day I walked into recovery, but I hadn't really listened or followed directions. I was simply treading water, heading somewhere (but I didn't know where), so I wasn't getting anywhere.

"Happy, joyous and free" still eluded me. My "family" had long since written me off, and so the people in the program became *my chosen family*. There was a group of about a dozen people who would gather for coffee after the meeting several times a week. I became close friends with one of the men in this group (who I began to date six months later). He worked a very strong program, and I began to be guided, taught, and encouraged by him and the others in the group to do simple things like letting go and letting God, living in the now, doing service work, and keeping it simple. Although I was somewhat stuck on Step One and the idea of a *loving God*, I was beginning to find just *that* in the program, and it gave me the chance to truly *surrender*.

As an abandoned child, I swore I would never ever leave one of my children. Yet, after two and a half years in recovery, I was forced into a dilemma: either give up these children to their father to raise, or lose my sanity entirely. This was one of the hardest things I had ever done in my entire life, and a physical demonstration that I had completely let go of *my will* in every area of my life. Through this process I became teachable and could finally see the ways in which my best thinking usually gave me results I didn't like.

I began to see that working with and trusting a higher power before I took action on anything afforded me a better chance of being restored to sanity. I'm not sure I'd ever had any real sanity in my life before that moment.

I was blessed with an opportunity to change professions and work in a field in which my boyfriend also worked. It required me to go out of state for six weeks of training, and if my children had still been in my care, I could not have taken this opportunity. The boyfriend had moved out of state, the children were gone to their dad's, and I no longer had to work two jobs. Today, I can see the gifts … but I sure couldn't then. I was truly alone for the first time in my life. It *had* to be God and me in all things now.

I did my first real Fourth-Step inventory during my training and took a hard look at how all my blaming of others had been an illusion. I prayed for the courage to be completely honest with God and myself and with the person who listened to my Fifth Step.

I wasn't immediately aware of the sense of freedom of having done my Fifth Step for about twenty-four hours, but when I woke up the next day, the world was literally brighter, and I wondered what was wrong with my eyes.

I had a real sense that up until that time, I had been living as though I were walking around under a wet wool blanket with little eyeholes cut in it. There was a euphoria that was clean and holy and one I never wanted to lose again. I realized that I had been living my life seeking out one person after another who would love me enough for me to feel whole, and if it wasn't a person, it was a substance, or both.

Becoming entirely ready to have my defects of character removed and humbly asking God to take and have all of me—the good and the bad—was an easy step at the time. Later, I would begin to see the depth of the meaning of Steps Six and Seven, which still lives with me today. Steps Eight and Nine were challenging in lots of different ways, but I made my list and became willing to allow the strength of God, through me, to take action and own my transgressions. Step Ten then began as a daily regimen, much like brushing my teeth and eating three meals a day and getting a little exercise and so forth.

> *I didn't so much admit I was wrong as I acknowledged you were right, or that my behavior, thinking, and actions had been harmful to others and myself. I no longer wanted to be an instrument of pain to anyone.*

It was quite some time before I felt comfortable with praying, and even a longer period of time before I felt comfortable trying to meditate. The Amish taught me that every thought is a prayer, so it was important to watch what I was thinking and to amend it when it was not what I wanted to think. I was also taught about pausing to appreciate all forms of nature—the simple love coming from a baby's eyes, the glorious dawn after a rainstorm—these were also forms of meditation. So, as it turns out, this short little Irish girl who hated God so desperately has fallen in love deeply and completely with God, as I *do not* understand it, but I don't need to anymore.

In conclusion, the boyfriend and I married, and we had twenty-three years together and two children in recovery. It ended year twenty-four, although we continue to be close friends and parents to the children who are now grown and all in Twelve-Step recovery, but one. In the program, I've weathered many difficult things, including the estrangement of my oldest daughter, the deaths of both mothers and fathers, and, closer to my heart, the deaths of very dear friends of many years in the program (none of which, thank God, were due to relapse). These Twelve Steps have changed me at depth, healing the wounds that brought me into the program and even healing wounds that I never knew existed.

Progress, Not Perfection

Before beginning the Twelve-Step program, I was easily flustered and discouraged, frequently upset with myself and my family. As a single mom, I worked full time and never felt like I had enough to give to my mom and daughter, who were living with me. Work wasn't going so great, either, and socially, I was either cutting off communications with other people or complaining too much when I did try to connect. There was a good amount of blame in my conversations and not much personal accountability. You might say it was a vicious cycle of negativity, as I was reaping what I had sown.

As I began working the steps, the most intimidating thing was the notion of doing an inventory and then going back to make amends with people. It seemed daunting, but my sponsor made it very clear how important this step was, and how important it was to do all the steps in a specific way.

I listened and soon learned the value of having a good coach. As we walked through my inventory, I was asked over and over again to state what my role was in holding onto pain, disappointment, insult, and injury.

What was I getting out of it? What was the payoff? It became clear that this work was a path to freedom of a sort, a precious type of freedom.

I had read other information about being present and living in the moment, but I have to say it was pretty impossible for me to do that without doing the Twelve-Step work. Getting through the middle steps opened things up for me. The best part was learning what to pray each night and each morning. Whenever I slip up and drop back into bad habits, I remember the starred and underlined passages in the notebook where I had written my Fourth Step. Remembering my Sixth and Seventh-Step prayers, this shows me exactly how to get back to basics, rely on my higher power, and focus on acknowledging and sincerely asking forgiveness for any behaviors and attitudes. In my Tenth-Step inventory, I find the shortcomings that I have still embodied to this day, as well as a process for corrective measures. This would be considered working my Tenth Step. Then, in the morning, praying sincerely to be shown how I can best serve is like getting a car to stop drifting off to one side. When I steer, I notice the car drifting out of the lane—my misguided attitude gives me a false sense of control. But when I seek guidance, it seems to stay aligned. This would be considered working my Eleventh Step.

I'm not perfect, but I know the steps provide a specific way to return at any moment to sanity and inner peace.

They allow me to choose to be a channel, vessel, transmitter, conveyor, and carrier of love who helps heal and support other human beings.

The transformative power of the Twelve Steps is that, forever, we have the tools, technology, and keys to access joy, peace, and contentment. This frees me from trying to be in control. For the first time in my life, I can open up to go with the flow, see what the day brings, and not get crazily stressed. I can actually relax and enjoy my days. I no longer disappear into a void and stop communicating with others. Sure, I need a little quiet time, but it isn't because I feel bad about myself or how things went the last time I spoke with someone. I'm quicker to own up to bad choices of words and behaviors and to apologize and make amends to clear the air. It feels so much better to operate this way. This is me working Steps Nine and Ten.

I still have to work on the "letting go and letting God" concept. Some days, I hold onto stuff too tightly for too long. Thank goodness there is a better way—specifically, using the steps to reconnect to my higher power. I am ever thankful for my sponsors who guided me through this process and opened my world to a higher quality of life, connecting with people and keeping the God channel open. God bless!

She Found Life's "Owner's Manual"

I began an extraordinary journey of recovery on March 11, 1987. At the time, I had no idea what a life-altering experience this would be; nor did I know that it would be my journey to freedom from bondage of self. I never dreamed it would be possible to like myself in my own skin. It's the greatest thing that has ever happened to me, and my gratitude makes me want to scream from a rooftop, but I don't—helping others is how I do this.

When I look back on my life before the Twelve Steps, it seems like I might as well have been living in a dark room, although I didn't know it at the time. I had confined myself to the world as I knew it and the messages I had unfortunately received. All I was aware of was the feeling of hopelessness and of not mattering to anyone. I believed I was a mistake, and the loneliness and ache in my heart was a plague I could never find a solution to.

Deep inside my soul, I always knew that God hadn't put me here to live the life I was living and that there had to be something better—I just didn't know what it was at the time. I never dreamed the answers to my loneliness and problems would come in the form of the Twelve Steps. For this reason, I always remember that no matter how long I have been in recovery, there's always something I don't know. This keeps me teachable.

My "something better" that I was so desperately searching for in every self-help book I could find began when I walked into the program for the first time, and I heard people talking about the way I felt. I didn't know that other people had the same feelings! It was an eye-opener for me. I suddenly felt the sense of *belonging* that I had sought for thirty-one years. I was finally validated. I went all the way in the program and sat all the way down, and I haven't found it necessary to leave since. Recovery has been a re-birth for me—a life I never dreamed I could have. Yet, I wouldn't change one stupid thing I did before recovery, or I might not have ever made it through the doors of the program!

Now, my experience can be useful in a way that no other formula can be to help the precious lives of others.

Before I came into the program, I had no instructions for living life. I was all over the map, a chameleon changing colors depending on who I was around. Now, I have some guidelines and have learned over time what boundaries are. As a result of having boundaries, I have gained respect from others—and myself. Nobody wants to be around someone who is a doormat, and I was once exactly that.

I can never begin to tell you what this program has done for my life! I found everything I was looking for and much more: I have joy in my life, even when things aren't always going the way I want them to.

I know now that whatever happens in life is going to bring strength and wisdom on the other side and that God definitely has a plan for me. My thinking got me in the door and will take me back out if I don't continue on this path, practicing my daily spiritual maintenance. I began to grow and know what true happiness and joy really are. The people in the program carried me and loved me until I could begin loving myself, and it has been my mission to pay back what I received.

A sponsor once told me to "turn up the volume of love," and I was so fascinated by that phrase that I started thinking of a way I could do that. My solution and mission became getting to know every person who walked through the doors of the program and asking them questions about their lives. People early in recovery usually love to talk about themselves. It's magical because most of us weren't ever listened to growing up! There is always a miraculous connection that is made when I do this, and I continue this *work* because it makes these broken people feel loved and cared for, which most of us had never genuinely felt before.

My life was spared, and it is my heart's desire to love every newcomer into loving him or herself, the way I was loved. It's a debt that I will always gladly pay forward, and also I get to reap the benefits of getting out of self! As long as I'm not in self, I know that something wonderful will happen.

It is my prayer that all who are seeking recovery will find their way into the loving arms of Peoples Anonymous and experience life for the first time!

A New Freedom

I was never enough. I wasn't big enough. I wasn't tough enough. I lost my first fight over sandbox turf to a five-year-old girl who had three mean older brothers and knew how to land a punch. In grade school, I was the last person chosen to play on any team. Although I was the spelling bee champion every year, it didn't help me on the playground.

As an outsider, my dearest dream was to be a part of the in-crowd. Popularity was more than a goal; it became an obsession. Somehow, I got the idea if I was elected to things, I'd be invited to the right parties and get respect from the tall, good looking, and secure.

As a result of this delusion, I was nice to everyone, whether I liked them or not. I was always campaigning for acceptance. On the surface, it paid off. I was elected vice president of the ninth grade, president of the tenth grade, and vice president of the student body. I was voted "Friendliest" in my senior class, though that title should have been "Most Desperate to Please." In college, I upped my game and was voted head cheerleader as a junior and president of the student body as a senior. By some miracle, I pledged the best fraternity—the one with a Wimbledon tennis champion as a member. In addition, I wrote and directed the school's variety shows, got a teaching certificate, and managed a B average by cramming for tests with friends who took notes. Somewhere along the line, I realized I was gay, but it was the early sixties, and that word hadn't been coined. My sexual orientation was my deepest secret and caused me to delve into fantasy and spend more time in the shower than necessary. In my grandiosity, I actually believed that if people found out I was homosexual it would be broadcast on the nightly news. After all, society told me I was a degenerate, and I bought that lie. I dated the best-looking girls to prove my heterosexuality to any doubters. Naturally, I chose those who were religious and wouldn't be expecting sex. My first job after college was teaching social studies at a multiracial junior high in Los Angeles, and I was good at it. My imagination and sense of humor worked for students from a variety of backgrounds. The administration offered me honors classes and a bright future. I was a success, but it wasn't enough. My addiction to approval had morphed into a need to be rich and famous. Being respected and well-liked was not enough for me. I had to be known and loved by millions of strangers.

After two years, I quit my job and moved to Manhattan with $500. My plan was to study acting and become a star. That I had no real background in acting and there were fifty thousand other wannabes pursuing a tiny number of jobs didn't deter me. I was special. I also decided it was time to stick one toe out of the closet. For the first time, I walked into a gay bar and used my real name. I discovered that there were four million men in New York City, and a good number of them wanted to have sex with me. It was the Age of Aquarius—a sexual Disneyland—and I made up for lost time. At twenty-three, I began a five-decade long trip into sexual addiction—a term that didn't exist for another fifteen years.

Over the next ten years, to finance my acting classes, voice lessons, and rent, I worked as a waiter, office temp, housecleaner, bartender, dog walker, apartment painter—and began to do some writing. My first article was printed on the Op-Ed page of the most prestigious newspaper in the country, then bought by the largest circulation magazine. That byline was an adrenaline shot to my ego. I was on my way! My next twenty submissions were rejected.

I knew no bounds in my quest for celebrity. I auditioned for every TV quiz show running and managed to get on a lot of them. I had my "fifteen minutes of fame" seven times! Once, I was a single question from winning $10,000 to $40,000 in today's money—and blew it. I came home with $3,300, furious that I'd failed.

Acting wasn't getting me where I wanted to be, so I wrote a book and sold it to a national publisher. I used connections to get myself booked on a top-rated network TV show to promote my masterpiece. The interview went so well that I got six minutes of airtime, triple the two minutes most authors get. With that national exposure, I was certain to make the bestseller list. To my dismay, the publisher hadn't gotten my book in many stores and the window of opportunity slammed shut. Not to be denied my destiny, I created a comedy act with a brilliant young actress. We won a talent contest and were invited to appear at New York's top improvisational comedy club. We shared the stage with current stars and future luminaries. There was only one catch: they got on when there was a full house, while we appeared at 3:15 a.m. for an audience of six drunks.

Then, our luck changed. We got a manager who sent our comedy sketches to the producer of a new ninety-minute live comedy show that was premiering in the fall. He called us into his office at 30 Rock and told us he loved our material and offered us a slot on his writing staff. After seven years, finally I had hit the big time! The producer said he'd call us the next month when the writers would start working. The weeks went by. Our manager called. We called. Nothing. We never heard from the producer again. The show went on to become an iconic hit that is still running on Saturday nights. It created many a star, but I was not one of them.

Within a year, I quit show business and resigned myself to being a nobody. I was thirty-three years old and tired of borrowing money from my parents and living hand-to-mouth. I called my entire address book and admitted that I was looking for a "real" job. Amazingly, I got one as a writer in the world headquarters of a Fortune 500 corporation. I was making good money for the first time in my life, but felt despondent that my shot at fame was gone. Even when I found in-house glory by writing speeches for the CEO and coaching him to become a good speaker, it did not satisfy my megalomania. When our company hired the most famous comedian in America to entertain at a conference for three thousand sales managers, I wrote a monologue for the megastar about the real issues his audience faced. He didn't understand one of my inside jokes, but agreed to do the first line. He said that if it got a big laugh he'd do the entire monologue. The line brought down the house and he did all my jokes. This was my moment! I was certain he would ask me to join his writing staff in gratitude for my brilliance. I never saw him again.

Just as I'd made a name for myself in the company and was offered a big raise and a chance to write for the CEO, I sold my co-op, took the money, and moved back to L.A. to try one more time to make it—this time as a TV writer. Much to my surprise, the industry was not eagerly awaiting my return. Instead, I started getting work as a speechwriter and coach. Over the next ten years, I developed a thriving career, worked with top executives, traveled the world, bought a house on a hill, had lots of money in the bank, and managed to hold together a five-year relationship. From the outside, it looked as if I had it all, but it didn't feel that way inside. I wanted more sex, more escape, more ego gratification. More was my motto. I walked away from my third good relationship in ten years due to a crippling inability to be faithful. I would meet a wonderful, caring person, win his heart, and tell him that I loved him. Then I'd withdraw my affections when I realized it meant living up to my word. My selfishness and deceit were as boundless as my need for approval. After my last self-induced breakup, I began to use drugs to amplify my sexual highs. Of course, I was still going to church, singing in the choir, and keeping the dark side of my life hidden from my friends and family.

It was as if I was back in college, once again living a double life and trying to pretend to be someone I wasn't.

Battered by bad choices and a belly full of pain, I started going to meetings and made my first attempt at working the steps. I identified as an alcoholic just so I could be in the rooms, though drinking was not my problem.

> *I suffered from a total inability to live life on life's terms. Selfishness, self-seeking, resentment, and fear were the soundtrack of my life. My problem was not an external substance but an internal malady.*

I had no daily connection with God and could feel my soul slipping away.

In the steps, I'd been given a recipe for a new life but didn't know how to use it. The map I'd been searching for all of my life was in my hands, but I couldn't read it. I worked the steps over and over again but didn't commit to doing them precisely as written. I went to hundreds of meetings, heard great speakers from around the country and told myself I was on the right path. I wasn't even aimed in the right direction.

As I hit one of those big zero birthdays, after decades of half-measures and false starts, finally, I'd had enough. I became willing to work the program one more time—as written. I found a larger-than-life sponsor who stuck with me through thick and thin. We went through the steps page-by-page, phrase-by-phrase, line-by-line. It took many months, but gradually, my ego began to shrink, my selfishness subsided, and I began to feel some peace. It was not a familiar feeling, but I've grown to appreciate it.

There was no lightning bolt of enlightenment, no sudden surge of serenity. In fact, I found that serenity doesn't surge; it sneaks up on you. Slowly, I surrendered my need to be anything more than I am. I admitted my powerlessness and turned my life and my will over to the care of God.

This time, I worked the steps exactly as directed and did not skip or skim or hold back on anything. I did an unsparing inventory of my past, holding nothing back, and shared it with my sponsor. I made amends to each person I had harmed, and this time, I asked if they had anything they'd like to say to me. Some had been waiting years for that opportunity, and I listened.

I do a daily devotional and meditation in the morning and a nightly review before I go to bed. I'm learning to stop when I feel fearful or agitated and ask God or another person in recovery for help. I am looking forward to sponsoring others, and I know that they will show up when the time is right. I'm no longer trying to manage my recovery; I'm letting my higher power do the heavy lifting. As a result of doing the steps exactly as directed, I haven't envied anyone in a long time. I've been delivered from fear, resentment and lust, one day at a time. At an age when most people are slowing down or retired, I'm starting to live fully for the first time. I no longer practice acceptance speeches for awards I don't need to win. To my amazement, being a member of the fellowship is more fulfilling than trying to rise above the crowd. I'm accepted for who I am, just as I accept others without comparison or reservation.

My goal is no longer to be rich and famous, but to support myself, help others, and serve God. That may mean making coffee, chairing meetings, telling my story, giving someone a ride, or reaching out to those in need. Today, I understand that acts of love and kindness are their own reward. They do not require applause. There is no trophy for humility, no spotlight for selflessness. Any time I can get out of myself and focus on the needs of others, I'm where I want to be. On my best days—and I have more and more of them—I see the promises of the program coming true in my life and the lives of others. I know a new freedom that I never found in my endless quest for fame and riches.

Today, I'm happy as I am, where I am, and look forward sharing my recovery with others.

While I have plans for the future, I do my best to stay anchored in the present. I've spent a lifetime trying to get "there." Today, I realize there is no *there*: only here and now. The present moment is where I want to be, and I am happy to report, it is really fun just *being me*! Working the Twelve Steps precisely and applying the spiritual principles to my life daily has given me this gift and so many more. I am very grateful for the gift of Peoples Anonymous to the human race.

Transformation

When I was young, I loved to look at the beautiful sky, the trees, and mother nature. This was the time of my life when all was well with the world, and I am grateful to have these moments in my memory.

By the time I was eleven, that all began to fade away. Once, there was an ominous tornado within three hundred yards of me and my friends—we were so intoxicated, we did not run away. We just stood there, mesmerized, thinking, "Wow! That's cool!"

Somehow, twenty years passed until the next ominous moment of my life occurred on November 10, 1996: I was signing the titles to everything I owned away—mostly motorcycles—to my brother. My brother and I had never gotten along very well, so as I was giving him all of my stuff, he was somewhat confused. He saw how miserable I was, consumed by the mental torture of what seemed to be inescapable hopelessness, worthlessness, and a constant feeling of impending doom.

During the twenty years of madness, I'd had three children, and none of their mothers would speak to me. I didn't have a car or a bank account and had resigned to the prison I had built myself. I genuinely believed I was going to be living this hopeless existence until the day I died; I had given up on life. Actually, I really wanted to die because I believed that everyone would be better off without me.

One day, my brother took me to a bookstore called Serenity West and said, "You need to talk to this guy named Rob." (At the time, I didn't realize it was going to turn out to be one of the nicest things my brother had done for me in years).

I was not expecting to hear that, but I did as he said. Coincidentally, Rob wasn't even supposed to be working on Sunday, but there he was, and we talked for hours. We each shared our stories with one another, during which I learned that twenty years earlier (while I was standing there facing the tornado), Rob was being taken in by a group of nuns after living on the street for a long time. He was housed in a church and sent to a Twelve-Step recovery meeting in the basement. While I sat there enthralled with his story of healing and transformation through working the Twelve Steps, I thought: *If this guy can do it, maybe I can, too.* My new friend took me to my first Twelve-Step meeting, and I honestly don't remember anything that happened there, except that I was informed in no uncertain terms by a guy named Charlie, "You do not have to live this way anymore."

I remember thinking, *How could he know how I have been living?* I flashed back to when I was about six. My family and I "visited" my grandparents for Christmas, and for me, the visit lasted five years—my father said he was going to the store and never came back. That really hurt. My grandmother, fortunately, was a kind and funny person who always would make us laugh. We had an understanding; as soon as I stopped squirming and laughing, she would get the splinter out of my foot. I always knew she had my best interests at heart.

I ended up getting into trouble with the law around age eleven. I'd stayed out way past dark and got caught "loitering." One day, I was asked by a close friend to help fix his motorcycle and found out the hard way it was stolen. I was arrested and they tried to send me to juvenile prison. My sweet grandfather got the call in advance and gave me warning that they were coming to get me, so I ran off. He told me, "Son, there's nothing I can do to help you."

I left home and joined a gang of approximately eight older kids who I called "The Clan." They were all much older than I was, between eighteen and thirty. We kept moving from place to place, probably because they didn't have money to pay the rent. We would steal, smoke marijuana, and drink booze, pretty much all day every day. This was our way of life.

By the time I was sixteen, I had my first son. His mom and I started spending time together when I was about twelve and she was nearly twenty (my sponsor later called that rape—but I didn't understand that until I was about forty-five). Due to our age difference and many other factors, my name was never placed on the birth certificate. I was informed that my son's mother would get in trouble if we told them I was the father.

I got a job pouring concrete from 6:00 a.m. to midnight. When I got home, I often fed my son, because his mother didn't seem to be able to feed him at night. When she left unexpectedly, I started raising him on my own: I enrolled him in school, karate, Little League—but I did not have custody, so whenever his mom didn't approve of something I did, she'd take him away from me. This happened quite often mid-semester of school, and many times, they did not have food, a place to live, electricity, etc. I tried to tell her he belonged somewhere where he could have these things, but my son loved his mother, and he always ended up going with her.

Eventually, she moved to San Francisco, convincing my thirteen-year-old son—in the middle of the school year—to take a Greyhound bus and join her in California. Soon, he called me from there, asking me to buy him a ticket back. I did. Shortly afterwards, his mom was pushed off a building and died. Her boyfriend called and gave the news to my son about his mother's demise.

Around the same time, I had my second child, a beautiful little girl. I was helping a friend move, and by chance, I ran into an old friend from grade school. She waited for me to finish helping the guys move and asked if we could get some wine. I said, "Sure."

She then asked, "If I get drunk, can I stay with you tonight?"

I agreed, and she stayed for three months before leaving suddenly. Five months later, I noticed a bump on her tummy. I asked, "Are you pregnant?"

She said, "No."

Three months later, I saw her again. The bump was larger, and once again I asked, "Are you pregnant?"

She said, "No."

A month later, I got a call saying she'd given birth to a baby girl and I was the father. My daughter was taken in by her aunt and uncle, who were a little more trustworthy than her mother, and for several years, they let me visit most birthdays, Christmases, and holidays. I was never allowed to tell her that I was her father, but when she was about four, she looked at me and said, "This guy really looks familiar. I think we look alike!" That's when her adoptive parents broke off contact with me and refused to answer my calls.

One year after my daughter was born, I had my second son. I was very excited to raise him, but in my condition at the time, I could not seem to show up as the father I really wanted to be to any of my children.

After these experiences, I had never thought less of myself. I was a bad father, a bad son, a bad everything. I was showering every eight or ten days.

Then, at my first Twelve-Step meeting, I felt hope for the first time in over twenty years.

My favorite thing about recovery has been genuinely reconnecting with my children and caring for my grandmother. Before working the steps, even if my family wanted to talk to me, I never had anything good to report. But after working the program, I became very close with my family and my grandmother. She really thought it was cool to watch me give stuff away instead of taking things from the world. She was very proud of me, and she even came along to about a hundred Twelve-Step meetings. My amazing mother was also extremely proud of me, and this made me feel really good in my heart. I worked the Twelve Steps of the program and began to trust God, clean up my mess, and make amends for my past. These days, not just my family members, but almost all the people I run into, especially those I build things for, express pride and gratitude. That was not my experience prior to working the steps. Best of all, I married a dazzlingly beautiful, kind woman who shares a life of adventure and fun with me!

My favorite thing to do is draw smiley faces on stuff. Really, I do it all the time. There is a ukulele hanging on my wall: dark yellow, with a big smiley face painted on it. I have worked in construction many years of my life. I have hung many ukuleles for a man who owns a music store, but this one I bought for myself.

Not everything that's happened in my life over the past twenty years in the program has come with a smile painted on it. Many of the friends I used to know have passed away or are in exactly the same place they were twenty years ago. My brother, the one who first saved my life by taking me to the little Twelve-Step bookstore, was imprisoned for his third DWI this past year. Recently, after my grandmother passed, I watched a pair of lawyers talk their way into keeping about two-thirds of my grandmother's estate for themselves, leaving my father with just a small portion.

I was definitely angry and upset. But, deep down inside, I knew that no matter what happened in life, I would never be left empty-handed. Nothing can take from me the memories that my grandmother and I made, not even the attorneys. When things don't go my way, I'm able to think, "Well, this is preparing me for the future." During this battle with the lawyers and my grandmother's estate, my awesome wife, while I was going through this struggle, drew even closer.

Working the Twelve Steps of the program of recovery transformed my life beyond anything I could have ever previously imagined. I live a life today of abundance, joy, prosperity, and happiness. I can directly attribute every blessing in my life somehow to working the Twelve Steps and to God.

In the future, I'd like to start an organization that digs wells for people in villages without access to clean, fresh water. I've been meeting people who I want to put together as a team, and I've started to see this plan coming together. The program has taught me, the more I give, the more I receive. It's funny, I seem to find money all the time, just lying on the ground—a $10 bill here, a $20 bill there. This also did not happen prior to me coming into the program. I'm sure that's just a coincidence. When I find the money, I can't find someone quickly enough to give it away to!

I learned that in the past, when I used to engage in any of my "coping" behaviors, such as using alcohol or drugs, or sex, or anger, it stopped me from growing. I have found one of the most powerful ways to cope with anything that comes into my life through applying the Twelve Steps to the problem and allowing God to help me grow through it.

The Luck Ran Out

I was born to an uneducated single parent whose three very enthusiastic boys all had high hopes of someday becoming productive members of society.

I'm the middle child, and ever since I can remember, I felt I lacked the attention I saw my older and younger brothers receive from my mother. So, growing up in poverty and struggling with not getting the attention I thought I should have, I reached out to the people in the neighborhood who would give me the attention I wanted through friendship. Usually, these people weren't on my side unless they needed someone to be available for their benefit.

Over time I wised up to this behavior and made my way into the sports scene, which helped me become semi-accepted. I enjoyed life well into my teens.

During this time, I started learning about the pros and cons of growing up as a black man in this country. When I graduated high school, I instantly joined the military. I believed this experience would give me direction and maturity; however, my first duty station was overseas and all that did was make me homesick. After spending what felt like countless years getting into relationships and hoping they would improve me, or fill that huge hole in my soul, I found myself trapped in a dead-end lifestyle that I would live for many years.

After getting in and out of jail, losing good jobs, and being unable to love myself or others, it became evident that I was running from reality, unwilling to accept the fact that I was living selfishly and without any morals.

Then, one day, a friend asked me for help moving. I instantly thought to myself, *No way*, but something deep inside of me said, *Stop being selfish and help somebody*. So I did, and that decision changed the direction of my life. It was the start I needed to get off the streets and get into a position where I could be introduced to the Twelve-Step program of action, which has transformed my life completely.

Living my life the way I thought I needed to, I ran out of luck. I ended up homeless and in fear of what terrible situation was going to happen next. Today, I'm truly grateful that God is my director and I'm his student. Through working the Twelve Steps, everything in my life today happens in accordance with the precise instructions laid out in this book.

I know today that there's no such thing as luck—only the protection and divine grace that we all receive from a loving higher power who I choose to call God! All my thanks go to his omnipresence, which I continue to trust wholeheartedly today and every day. Recovery has given me so many blessings, more than I could even begin to count. My life is full of joy, beauty, and grace. As a direct result of working the Twelve Steps, I am living, loving, and laughing all the way to the bank—the spiritual bank, that is! I give thanks to all those who have helped me along the way: because of them, my account is full.

God Has No Other Hands But Ours

G rowing up, I was spoiled and overindulged; yet, at the same time, I never felt I was getting the attention I needed and deserved. My siblings, three sisters and one brother, were all more beautiful than I was, and my mother wasn't shy about letting me know it.

"Can't you do something with that hair?" she would ask.

Some days, it was: "Are you really going to have that second piece of pie?"

As a young girl, I thought about becoming a nun. My aunt on my dad's side was a nun, and I thought it would be so beautiful, so mysterious, to devote myself to God in that way—but my mother said, "You wouldn't know a calling from God if He grabbed you by the hair."

I hated her for saying these things to me, and I believed she was responsible for how badly I started to feel. Even as a little girl, I'd sit in the dark and cry all the time. The whole world was against me; even the things that seemed positive at first would turn black before my eyes. For instance, a friend of mine had a mother who always called me "Bella," which means "beautiful." How I adored being called "Bella!" But some time later, at her funeral, her son reminisced about the way she would always call any girl who came over "Bella," because she couldn't remember any of our names. That hit me hard.

I got through life by designing an elaborate series of masks. One of my first was for daddy: that was the "sweet, good little girl" mask, and I thought it was working splendidly, especially when daddy took me aside and told me, "There is no one more important in my life than you." (In fact, only twelve years ago, I learned that he had done the same thing for all four of my other siblings). To say the least, I got good at *seeming*, on the outside, like nothing was wrong.

Actually, on the outside, nothing was wrong. My daddy, born on the island of Galveston, had always felt poor, so when he grew up, he went to law school and decided that his family would never want for anything. My daddy tried with all his might never to let us kids see any suffering or misery. Despite that, in eighth grade, I went to Mexico on a school trip and saw poverty for the first time. *People have TVs outside, and no floors!* I realized in horror. *The children are half naked, begging!*

This experience, however, didn't change my outlook, and I was perpetually consumed with self-centered problems. I never felt good enough, and I expressed that by trying to do everything perfectly: if I vacuumed and someone walked on the carpet, I'd vacuum again just to get rid of that one shoe print. I ironed shirts until they didn't have even a hint of a crease, and if I hung them and they wrinkled, I ironed them again. God forbid it if I ever turned in an essay with an eraser mark on it—I rewrote every page until it was perfect. When I graduated high school and even started college, it still seemed like nothing was wrong on the outside.

After high school, some bad things happened that I couldn't ignore. At nineteen, I met a thirty-six-year-old man and married him immediately: I wore a see-through blue gauze dress to court, and when the judge said, "For better or for worse," I said, "For better!"

That was the worst thing I could have done. The marriage was a nightmare that, fortunately for both of us, lasted only two months. I remember walking into the bedroom, where my husband hit me in the face. When I saw my blood on the floor, and I realized, *That is my blood,* I remember thinking that I hated this man. I wanted to kill him.

I had never thought that before about anybody. Suddenly, my twelve years of religious education rushed in and told me that if I killed somebody, that would be the clincher: I was definitely going to Hell. I was already convinced that I would go to Hell, because there were only Ten Commandments, and I couldn't obey them. I lived in fear. I even had a mental image of myself in Hell: a very old, wrinkled woman in a little red rocking chair, with a jug of wine on my left, a bong on my right, and a rosary in my lap. I had made some peace with that image, because I thought it was inevitable.

I escaped that marriage by way of an affair with the man who would become my second husband. We got married because we were friends and we both had dreams, not for any of the right reasons. Before we married, he encouraged me to have a baby, my first son, despite the fact that I had conceived him with someone else. My husband was in love with that baby, but just days after my second son was conceived, he got another woman pregnant and said he didn't want to be married to me anymore. This was mostly all right with me; I had never been able to form a strong relationship, and even from a young age, my friends had always asked me how "boyfriend du jour" was doing. So, I moved in with my mother and started to raise my son.

This would have been a recipe for disaster in the best of cases, but it made things worse when my son, from an early age, turned out to be a mini-me. Like me, he wanted everyone to pay attention to him all the time, and he didn't care what kind of attention it was. Like me, he was full of darkness. By the time he was two, he was throwing tantrums that involved throwing chairs and beating his head against the wall, and I had to sit outside so the neighbors didn't think I was beating him. Soon after, he was getting in trouble in school, and when he didn't get what he wanted, he would light fires in his bedroom. I tried to take him to the doctor, but he rarely took his medication, and he would threaten to open the car door on the highway on the way to his appointments. He hated himself, which made him hate me, and I hated myself, and all the hate made me hate him, and there was no way out. It's agonizing, as a mother, to realize that you hate your child. This was destroying me utterly.

Meanwhile, his little brother, three years younger, was one of those kids who would just run around the living room whistling. Nothing bothered him. Things would just roll right off his back, and I felt like God had given me one who needed me and one who needed nothing at all. Of course, my younger son did need me, and I went to all his sports games (even though I didn't always root for the right team). I knew this wasn't enough, but I felt like it sucked all the air out of my lungs just trying to make his older brother happy. Most weekends, I went out, leaving my mother to wonder if I'd ever make it home, and what would she tell my boys if I didn't?

"That's enough fun for one day," she would tell me. For years, I didn't see how there could ever be enough fun.

At last, when my older son was seventeen and considering joining the army, explicitly so that he could get himself killed, I hit bottom. I needed to find a way out, or death would come for one or both of us. I started going to Al Anon meetings (gatherings for friends and relatives of alcoholics) because I needed a place to unload the pain I was feeling. I would go to those meetings, and I would cry and cry and cry and cry. When I eventually decided to work the steps myself, Peoples Anonymous didn't exist, but I always understood that I wasn't seeking recovery from alcoholism, specifically. I needed to heal.

Right away, interesting things started to happen. The first person I wanted as my sponsor rejected me: she said she thought we could have too much fun together, and we'd both relapse. These days, we're friends—we have a secure bond through our mutual love of gardening—but at the time, that rejection was hard for me. However, I soon found this little old lady who was loud, red-haired, and reminiscent of Brunnhilde from the Valkyrie comics. She seemed like she would kick my ass, and I needed that. She was also a little crazy, so we saw eye to eye.

I dipped my toes into my First Step. I already believed in God, so that part was easy, but I still didn't fully accept my personal powerlessness. After all, I had raised two sons, I'd never been fired, and my many masks seemed to be fooling everybody. Nobody had ever looked at me and said, "You look sad." So, even though I was crushingly sad, I felt like I was in control. Add to that the fact that I could steal with ease—usually little things that I could have easily paid for—while wearing my "she would never steal a thing" mask.

Still, I felt like I could keep going through the steps. When my sponsor told me that I could create a God of my own understanding, I felt something really powerful. I made this really, really handsome God who looks like a cross between my daddy, Dean Martin, and Elvis. He loves me so much, and takes me into His arms, and forgives me even before I do anything, because He knows I don't mean to. He gave me a great deal of strength.

When it came time to make my amends, the hardest one was to my mother. I had been so horrible to her for so many years, but all she said to me was, "Well, I thought it was my lot in life to suffer with a daughter like you. No worries."

That drove me crazy! She was like a martyr with Christ-like forgiveness, and it let all the wind out of my balloon, when I had really wanted her to just pop it. I wanted her to be angry with me, because I deserved it, and in some ways, because that would justify the way I'd hated her.

In later recovery, I realized that my mother had done her best raising me with the tools she had, and I had, too, with my own children—nobody's perfect, and it didn't make sense to blame her or myself for making mistakes. In fact, recovery was the first time I learned that there was no such thing as perfection—that was a tremendous weight off my shoulders! I also learned that feelings are not facts, and every time I have a feeling, like "Ugh, I am my mother!" or every time I feel fear (usually of losing something I have, but sometimes of not getting something I want),

I know that the feeling is not a fact, and I have a proven way of getting through it.

I even know how to help others get through their feelings. My favorite is my four-year-old grandson: sometimes, he'll come over, and I'll sense a little negativity or irritability. My strategy is to declare a laugh-a-thon, which means we make each other laugh and laugh and laugh and laugh, and before you know it, the would-be meltdown is long forgotten. (By the way, laughing until you cry is a cure for the blues that is safe for all age groups).

Before recovery, I struggled with self-confidence and with saying no. Saying no was difficult because it meant I wasn't perfect, or I wasn't good enough, and I was constantly wiped out as a result of my inability to admit when it was all too much. Now, I not only can say no with ease; I can say yes! Once, I noticed an advertisement seeking a blonde actress to play some minor role. I had always wanted to be an actress, so I decided to show up and audition, even though I most certainly am not blonde. I never got a callback, but the thrill and the joy of just going for it and the purity of that caution-to-the-wind adrenaline rush still brings a huge grin to my face.

I feel the closeness to God that I wanted to feel as a little girl, when I thought I wanted to become a nun. I know some people in recovery who don't drink communion wine, and I understand that choice, but when I take communion, I feel deeply connected to the Catholic tradition that once the wine has been blessed by the priest, it has literally become the blood of Christ. Nothing could be further from my mind in that moment than the idea that this union with God could jeopardize my recovery in any way. (I am certainly not advocating this for anyone suffering from the disease of addiction, but it just happens to be my experience).

Every day, I live by the Dorothea Solle quote: "God has no other hands but ours." For example, when my father had a stroke, my siblings and I decided not to put him into a nursing home. We alternated taking care of him each week. As a grown woman, it felt strange to begin to bathe my naked father—but I believe that God helped me through that experience, making me feel that this was the body of Christ, and the service I was giving to my father was going directly to God. As a drug and alcohol educator, I try to share the love of God with my students, and I feel close to God when that love starts to help soften the hard shell of someone who feels like the day will never end because it hurts so much just to be alive. Every day, I pray for things to end up the way God wants them to end up, and from where I'm standing, that looks a lot better than it ever did when I prayed for things to go the way I wanted them to.

The tiniest miracles amaze me the most. I once saw a teeny-tiny lizard—he must have been a newborn baby—and I thought, that was a miracle. I saw a baby praying mantis, too, and I felt a sunrise in my heart when I saw that. Before recovery, I would have never seen these things, and even if I had, I would have never appreciated them. Now, my life is full of growth, in and outside my garden, but I especially love the herbs I grow, because to me, *herbs* stand for "His Earth's Radiance By Son-light." And yes, both of my sons are all grown up, alive and well, and so are my relationships with them. Recovery was a life-saving blessing for me, and I'm excited that in the future, more people like me, regardless of what they seek to heal from, will be able to walk this path with joy in Peoples Anonymous.

Author's Note

I am very grateful to report: I am no longer interested in my own opinion. *My opinion* damn near killed me, therefore I *assuredly* would not share it with anyone I care about. Please do not allow some of my wild ideas, radical thoughts, and personal struggles along *my path* to keep you from doing the powerful work inherent in the exercises of the Twelve Steps.

I fully understand that this way of life may not be for everyone. There are many beautiful paths to a spiritual awakening; this is only one of them. Interestingly, it seems that many on the planet live the principles and ideas of the Twelve Steps instinctively.

As for the rest of us, it is usually when we have grown sick and tired of being sick and tired, agonizingly discontent with our attempt to treat the internal spirituality malady with external things, that we finally find our way into the program of Peoples Anonymous.

As the author of this work, it is my sincere desire to encourage the members of Peoples Anonymous to try to share only their experience, strength, and hope with others in the healing process. This means we usually do not speak on a subject that we have no *actual* experience with. Having read about something in a book or studied it in school does not meet this qualification, I'm afraid. Although education is extremely helpful, it also does not provide *the* necessary ingredient of *experience*. For example, we can study all there is to know about cancer, and we can have great love and compassion and an extreme desire to help those who are sick with it, we can even be very educated *about it* - but we can speak from experience with it *only* if we have had a doctor look in our eyes and give us the diagnosis. Those who have undergone *this* process and have lived through it can speak from a place of experience and wisdom. Wisdom, in our context, is experience successfully applied, resulting in a genuinely helpful outcome. We do not mean in any way to minimize the tremendous value of having a good doctor to walk us through the physical healing process, for this is absolutely essential in dealing with medical issues; we are simply acknowledging how *equally* priceless it would be to have someone also by our side who has actually healed from cancer and is willing to share with us precisely how they recovered based on his or her *experience*.

Metaphorically, this great gift of insight and *vast transformational wisdom* has been freely given us in Peoples Anonymous from the preceding twelve-step movements.

It may be interesting to note here that when you ask someone in the program for help, the person's first question is usually not "What type of insurance do you have?"

The dictionary defines *opinion* as: a belief or judgment drawn by someone that rests on grounds *insufficient* to produce complete certainty. A personal view, attitude, or appraisal.

I am sad to report that even with all the advances of consciousness the human race has made, there are still those who are busy sharing their *opinions* with any person or group of people in the world willing to listen, either face-to-face, through blogs, or in other media.

I, on the other hand, usually define opinion as: a person's ego elaborating verbosely on a topic it honestly has *no actual experience* with and therefore *really* knows nothing about.

We are addressing this vital truth about "the opinions of the world" here because—after I spent years working the Twelve Steps, after my life was radically transformed beyond my wildest dreams, after I became an extremely satisfied customer of the Twelve Steps, after they brought me more happiness, abundance, joy, and peace of mind than I could ever imagine, after they gave my life such meaning and purpose that it still brings me humbly to tears, *and* after I wrote a book on the subject—I googled AA, The Twelve Steps, and related keywords to *conclude* my research for the book.

For the first time in years, I encountered several extensive negative opinions about an extremely crucial and life-or-death matter coming from people who had absolutely *no actual experience* with what they were talking about. These opinions were clearly biased and distorted in the individuals' attempts to publicize their conclusions based solely on skewed observations.

Fortunately, I did this research *after* I worked the Twelve Steps, for if I had read these negative rants first—and if they had given me pause—then I, being a recovering alcoholic whose life truly depended on this Work, would surely be dead. I would have become a casualty of the irresponsible opinions of those who probably had *not sincerely worked the entire program precisely.*

As previously stated, blaming a recipe for not baking a delicious cake after only putting in half or three-quarters of the ingredients called for is as insidious as taking only half of your antibiotics for a serious infection and blaming the doctor when they fail to cure you. The Twelve-Step recipe, like any other recipe or prescription for that matter, must be followed precisely. We cannot over emphasize this enough, for possibly *only all the happiness in the world depends on it.*

The main empirical and intelligent way we, or anyone, can determine the "success rate" of working the Twelve Steps is to actually observe the entire process of a "test subject" and not only ensure that he or she has followed the instructions exactly but also *somehow* confirm each step was completed *sincerely.*

As common sense would surely dictate, no one has the ability to discern such a thing by observation; while we may be able to record someone's actions during each step, we assuredly cannot establish the earnestness and sincerity put into the application of each *essential direction* of the recipe.

Fortunately, there is a perfect test that provides indisputable evidence of the results of those who have worked the steps in the precise fashion they were designed: "You will know *them* by their fruit." The work itself bears the fruit necessary to demonstrate, without a shadow of doubt, the power inherent in the application of the spiritual principles of the Twelve-Step movement.

We have traveled the world; we have witnessed with our own eyes the literally countless lives transformed by working this program. There are no words to even begin to describe the beauty we have beheld.

We know it works. We have not only seen the fruit in our own lives but also we have had front-row seats to witness it *literally in millions of others.*

In writing *Peoples Anonymous,* we went to great extremes to acquire the permissions needed to copy many of the directions from the sacred writings of the Big Book of Alcoholics Anonymous in their entirety. The reason is, in all humility, I knew I could not even attempt to improve on a process that has worked so powerfully for so many. I simply wanted to make it available to the rest of the planet. I consider the information that originally came through Bill W. to not only be divine inspiration but also an answer to prayer for the healing of alcoholics then, and now, for the rest of our world.

The entire book and this profound Spiritual Technology can be distilled into it's purest form with six words: **Trust God, Clean House & Help Others**.

Abandon yourself to God as you understand God. Admit your faults to Him and to your fellows. Clear away the wreckage of your past. Give freely of what you find and join us. We shall be with you in the Fellowship of the Spirit, and you will surely meet some of us as you trudge the Road of Happy Destiny.

May God bless you and keep you-until then. (BB, p. 164)

Thank you AA, for helping to save my life and now possibly our world (who would have thought).

The Twelve Steps of Alcoholics Anonymous

1. We admitted we were powerless over alcohol—that our lives had become unmanageable.
2. Came to believe that a Power greater than ourselves could restore us to sanity.
3. Made a decision to turn our will and our lives over to the care of God *as we understood Him.*
4. Made a searching and fearless moral inventory of ourselves.
5. Admitted to God, to ourselves, and to another human being the exact nature of our wrongs.
6. Were entirely ready to have God remove all these defects of character.
7. Humbly asked Him to remove our shortcomings.
8. Made a list of all persons we had harmed, and became willing to make amends to them all.
9. Made direct amends to such people wherever possible, except when to do so would injure them or others.
10. Continued to take personal inventory and when we were wrong promptly admitted it.
11. Sought through prayer and meditation to improve our conscious contact with God, *as we understood Him*, praying only for knowledge of His will for us and the power to carry that out.
12. Having had a spiritual awakening as the result of these Steps, we tried to carry this message to alcoholics, and to practice these principles in all our affairs.

CPSIA information can be obtained
at www.ICGtesting.com
Printed in the USA
LVHW091124220919
631863LV00010B/252/P